BIG Birthdays

BIG
Birthdays

THE PARTY PLANNER CELEBRATES LIFE'S MILESTONES

David Tutera

PHOTOGRAPHY BY CHARLES AND JENNIFER MARING

BULFINCH PRESS
NEW YORK · BOSTON

Bulfinch Press

Time Warner Book Group

1271 Avenue of the Americas, New York, NY 10020

Visit our Web site at www.bulfinchpress.com

First Edition: April 2006

LIBRARY OF CONGRESS CATALOGING-IN-PUBLICATION DATA
Tutera, David.
Big birthdays : the Party Planner celebrates life's milestones / David Tutera ; photography by Charles and Jennifer Maring.
p. cm.
Includes index.
ISBN 0-8212-6172-X (hardcover)
1. Birthday parties. 2. Cookery. 3. Handicraft. I. Title.
TX731.T863 2006
793.2 — dc22

2005021124

Design by Vertigo Design NYC
PRINTED IN SINGAPORE

To my family and friends...

Thank you for celebrating the past forty years of my life with me.

No birthday would have been a milestone without you!

Contents

Introduction

It all began with a piñata and a dream. When I was growing up, my mother always threw the very best birthday parties in the neighborhood, and as far as I'm concerned, the world. She seemed to outdo herself every single year, dressing up familiar rooms with elaborate decorative themes, devising the perfect games and activities, coordinating fun and exciting menus and cake designs, and brainstorming super-smart color schemes for that extra flair. We looked forward to our birthdays for about three hundred and sixty-four days of the year, and I still remember every single one vividly. One early party stands out in particular, though. The candles on the cake were already lit, a dozen of my friends were cavorting around the room wearing party hats and big smiles, and I was standing beneath a piñata that had finally surrendered its loot. As it rained down candy and dime-store toys, I remember asking myself for the very first time, *Can I do this for a living someday?*

Lucky for me the answer was yes. It's been over twenty years since I started planning parties professionally, writing books on entertaining, like *The Party Planner,* and rescuing parties in distress on my own television show. And even though I travel all over the world designing events of all kinds and sizes for all types of clients — from celebrities like Star Jones and Susan Lucci to regular folks who just like to celebrate — party planning gives me the same amazing feeling I had at that birthday party so many years ago. Yes, the candy was a plus at the time, but it was really the combined sense of exhilaration, gratitude, ritual, and camaraderie and the creativity and care I recognized in all of my mother's efforts that made me want to do what I do.

Today, those same things make throwing birthday parties one of my very favorite projects. My career epiphany that occurred beneath that fateful piñata may not happen for everyone, but there's something about a birthday celebration, especially early in life, that resonates deep inside all of us. Unlike other special celebrations that I always look forward to planning — weddings, anniversaries, and parties honoring personal accomplishments — we celebrate birthdays from day one (literally!), and each one marks a milestone on life's way that gains more and more meaning. And unlike holidays — which I am, of course, a sucker for, too — birthday parties are all about the participants. Birthday parties are a quintessential celebration of the way we grow and change, of who we are, and of the loved ones who help us develop as time goes on. There are no mandatory customs other than the ones you choose — it's your party, and as the song says, you can even cry if you want to (though I *always* advise against it). To put it simply, there are as many kinds of birthday parties as there are people.

In this sense, the basic tradition of the birthday party is not so unlike a piñata. It can hold countless different treats and possibilities, and whatever you get, you know it will be fun and surprising. I help people plan birthday parties for themselves, for family members, as a surprise for friends, and even in celebration of group birthdays. Some of my clients want to celebrate with only their nearest and dearest in front of the family fireplace in the countryside of New England. Others want to surprise their loved one with a birthday boat trip down the coast of the Italian Riviera, where they'll meet friends along the way. I've also had clients like Dylan — whose twenty-fifth birthday party appears in this book — who

want hundreds of people to join them for cocktails and dancing in a hot New York club, dressed up just for them. The only absolute nonnegotiable rule for throwing a good birthday party is to put the honoree's interests above all others for one special day . . . and that's where I come in.

Translating someone's personality into the perfect birthday party can be a daunting task, especially for the really important milestone occasions like sweet sixteens and centennials. Even if a person's tastes and interests are well known, it can be hard to figure out how to make those details come to life in a particular setting, meal, or decorative scheme. That's why I've mapped out every single step that went into designing, planning, and constructing the ten great birthday parties that fill the pages of this book. I take you from the idea stage to the aftermath, breaking down each event into the five different senses — look, touch, scent, sound, and taste — that define the key elements of the party in both the imagination process and in actual experience. After all, it's never one thing that makes your birthday party unforgettable. It's the heat of the candles on your face just before you make a wish and the sweet, sticky taste of the perfect cake; it's the scale of the room and the colors that sweep through it; it's the sight of all your

friends smiling and the slick sheets of wrapping paper; it's the whole fantastic living moment that a simple date on the calendar can't quite express.

Of course, it's not just figuring out how to rouse all the senses that makes a birthday party great. People grow up, and their parties should do so with them. With this fact in mind, I've packed this book with an array of different milestone birthdays, spanning the ages from one to one hundred. The first two parties are for children, and they focus on balancing the whims of the little ones with the practical concerns of the parents, who also want to have a good time. (How can you meet the needs of a hungry one-year-old and a mother who wants to catch up with friends at a civilized afternoon gathering? Or throw a safe father-and-son fishing party for a gaggle of five-year-old boys and still enjoy a grown-up meal?) The next two parties are for young adults who are just figuring out who they are and enjoying their newfound self-determination.

The next group of parties covers those milestone birthdays when life finally takes shape: the thirtieth, fortieth, and fiftieth. Whether a former fraternity brother is hoping to bring more of a black-tie feel to his old beer-and-brisket days, or a newly single woman is looking for a balance between old traditions and fresh starts, these parties sketch a road map for celebrating one of life's most liberating moments: when you're finally a grown-up and you know what you want. The last three parties cover some of the most meaningful milestones of all, with honorees turning sixty-five, seventy-five, and one hundred years old. These parties unfurl the sprawling dreams of long, full lives in a variety of different ways — from transforming an ordinary suburban backyard into an exotic setting for an adventurous retiree to cooking up a perfect evening at home for a food-loving couple sharing a one hundredth birthday. As lovely and eclectic as the people they celebrate, these parties only confirm that birthdays get even better with age.

Using the parties described in this book as a sourcebook for ideas, a conceptual guide, or an exact blueprint will help you conceive and construct an amazing event. In the end, though, throwing a great birthday party is only partly in the planning. It's the passion, love, and wonder that the event sparks among the people paying tribute to the journey of life that makes the memory of a birthday party, like the memory of a certain piñata, last forever.

Chloe's 1st

A GIRLS' DAY OUT

for ten

If you've ever known a one-year-old, you know that the hope, wonder, and joy with which they discover the world is more than just a prelude to what they will become. Before baby even takes a step, one of the most important parts of life's journey — the beginning — has already taken place, and that definitely deserves a good party. Nevertheless, lots of parents don't know how to celebrate this pivotal first milestone. One question trumps all the others: why throw a party for someone who won't understand or remember it? (Maybe I've thrown too many parties for rock stars to worry about this particular problem.) The fact is that the basic ceremony of the first party is as important as anything else — like a ribbon-cutting ceremony for all the years of great birthdays to come.

When I met Racquel, the mother of a beautiful little girl named Chloe who was on the verge of turning one, she was already convinced that the ceremony was important. But she did have another common question: should the party be for the parents or the kids? Experience has taught me that the answer is: for both. At this age the little ones do not need a wealth of activities and toys so much as they need attention from adults, so the focus should begin with the latter. But with a little ingenuity, an appreciation for practicalities, and a sense of what the mothers and fathers might find fun and relaxing, you can throw a first birthday party that honors with simplicity and ease the true collaborative spirit of all first steps. For instance, after I learned that Chloe loved to play beneath the tall, shady trees in her backyard and that Racquel enjoyed meeting her girlfriends there for a monthly tea party, I thought it would be perfect to combine these two special treats into one. And once I found out about Racquel and her husband's prized collection of teddy bears — which for years had filled the room where Chloe now slept — I could see it all unfolding before me. White wicker chairs and rockers would be placed in between the pale pink personalized high chairs for a fresh and serene look that would lose nothing in durability, comfort, or proximity to mom. Perfect pink-and-white toile fabric with sophisticated accents of chocolate brown, a few casual frills, bright helium balloons, and no-fuss gingham would bring the cheerful glow of a modern Victorian girls' day out to both generations, while a centerpiece piled with pink and brown teddy bears tethered to pink, opal, and clear balloons would charm the younger set. The party would be a fun, special picnic with playmates and a few early tastes of gourmet cooking for Chloe and her pals, but also a civilized tea party to slow down the hectic pace of life for Racquel and her friends, and the beginning of a journey that none of them would ever forget.

Should the party be for the parents or the kids? Experience has taught me that the answer is: for both.

The princess and the teddy bear

IF MY EXPERIENCE working with moms has taught me anything, it's that raising a little toddler is not always a serene and precious experience. Chasing a speedy crawler, mixing baby food, and keeping enough distractions coming to fend off a caterwauling attack are more than a full-time job. For this reason, I wanted to make the environment for Chloe's party as calm as possible. The moms could enjoy a little escape for an afternoon while the babies were being enchanted by simple patterns and pretty decorations.

For the color scheme, I updated a classic baby-girl pink with a little chocolate brown. Why not indulge in spring fashion colors for a chic little girl? A beautiful invitation from Encore Studios featured a brown panel card with a beveled edge, pink type, and the image of a tiny teddy bear. I set a single round table (big enough for ten) with an elegant pink-and-white cotton cloth and a feminine toile-like pattern. The babies were seated in hand-painted wooden high chairs with pink-and-brown spokes. Each child's name was painted on a high chair seat in a loopy cursive script (a kind of *Laverne & Shirley* font, if you will!). Babies were treated to personalized and

embroidered bibs, while moms found personalized silver baby bracelets nestled in their napkins. I tied handwritten name cards around the necks of cute brown teddy bears that served as party favors, too. Polka-dot plates and pink-handled forks and spoons looked sweet and dreamy next to little pink-hued glasses. Dessert was served in white waffle-print ice-cream-cone dishes tied with pretty pink-and-white bows around the rims.

In the center of the table was a fabulous cluster of classic pink and brown teddy bears. A bouquet of opal, pink, and clear balloons spilled upward from the pile of bears. Striped and polka-dot ribbons in shades of pink and brown gussied up the bears and streamed from the hovering balloons. I positioned four more matching balloon clusters at the four corners of the party space. One of the most important pieces of the scene was a place of quiet repose. Sometimes a mom and a baby need to take a little quiet time together in a more private spot, so Victorian wicker furniture covered with comfy, soft teddy bears made for a perfect nursing and cuddling retreat just a few feet from the luncheon table.

My final decorative touch came in the form of a unique gift for Chloe. It's what I call a "Baby Time Capsule." This special gift was a box for photos and keepsakes to which Racquel could contribute for many years to come so that one day Chloe could look back on her life one birthday at a time.

Baby time capsule

MATERIALS

- round battery-operated clock with removable face
- 12 small Lucite boxes about the same depth as your clock (available at The Container Store)
- modeling glue or plastic glue
- colored marker or paint pen
- crystals, optional
- photograph of baby
- newspaper headline or clipping

METHOD

1. Remove the plastic face of the clock. (It should easily snap off.)

2. Using modeling glue, attach the Lucite boxes to the outside rim of the clock — one box at each of the twelve hours. Allow them to dry. (For additional accent, glue little crystals at each number, making sure to leave room to reattach the face.)

3. With a colored marker or pen, write the child's name on the center of the clock face.

4. Trim the photo to fit inside the Lucite box, fold the clipping, and insert them both into the box positioned at one o'clock. On each birthday thereafter, insert a photo and newspaper headline or clipping from that day.

5. Place the cover back on the clock.

the TEXTURE

Baby soft

USUALLY I PLAY UP THE CONTRAST OF TEXTURES in my parties, making sure never to go too severe or too soft. But for this delightful little girl's party, I went with soft all the way. After all, who needs severe when it comes to the cozy world of all things baby? Fluffy teddy bears were piled atop a soft cotton tablecloth, and creamy desserts filled smooth ceramic waffle-print dishes. Shiny satin ribbons adorned most of the decorative elements, while big, glossy balloons bobbed and bumped overhead.

Of course babies are not the only ones who like to be enveloped in ultrasoft blankets and cushions. Rumor has it that mommies like this kind of treatment, too. Since the first birthday is really a celebration for both mommy and baby, I made sure each guest was treated to a pampering touch. While the babies snuggled up to big velvety-soft teddy bears, the moms reclined on the deep-cushioned wicker sofa. While the babies enjoyed creamy organic yogurt, the moms relished dollops of delicious cupcake frosting. And while the babies practiced walking (and sometimes falling) on the soft garden lawn, the moms stood by, soothed by spoonfuls of cool raspberry sorbet.

HOW to Personalized baby blanket

This makes a wonderful party favor or personalized gift.

MATERIALS

○ digital photograph of baby

○ printable fabric

○ pinking shears

○ pink or baby blue blanket

○ heavy-weight thread and needle

○ ribbon

METHOD

1. Print the child's photo on printable fabric (available online or at a computer supply store).

2. Once it's dry, trim the photo with pinking shears.

3. Use a cross-stitch to attach the photo to the corner of the blanket.

4. Accent with a ribbon and tie it.

Think pink

IF PINK WERE A FLAVOR, I just know it would be sweet and delicate, and Racquel and I both agreed that the menu for the party should be both of those things. Need I even add that the color of every dish should be perfectly pink, too? But however frivolous you may want a first birthday party to be, you need to keep in mind user-friendliness and safety, too. Children as young as Chloe generally don't eat processed sugar, and their mothers seldom have more than one free hand, so I offered all sorts of small bites to satisfy everyone's appetite. For the babies I provided homemade applesauce, small jars of teething biscuits, puréed organic peas, and elegant little dishes of finger foods made especially for babies. For the moms I offered more elaborate delicacies.

I devised a selection of delectable desserts that included natural fruit concoctions for the babies and classic bite-size treats custom-made for moms on the go. While the little ones enjoyed homemade baby food — plain whole-milk yogurt blended with fresh organic raspberries — their beaming escorts spooned tart raspberry sorbet from old-fashioned white ice-cream-cone dishes and sipped herbal iced tea that added another punch of raspberry essence to the mix. Racquel and her girlfriends enjoyed the majesty, the playfulness, and the scrumptious vanilla taste of a three-tiered "cupcake cake," iced all in pink and assembled on stacked dessert plates to resemble a more formal confection by the fun-loving sweet-shop aficionados at Baked. In the end, I think the short set enjoyed looking at all those brightly colored pink treats almost as much as their mothers enjoyed eating them. And thanks to the recipe attached to each little jar of baby food with a tiny spoon and a swatch of fabric to match the table linens, they could do so together at home whenever a special occasion arose again.

the Menu

ORGANIC YOGURT AND
FRUIT BABY FOOD

TEETHING BISCUITS

HOMEMADE APPLESAUCE

RASPBERRY SORBET

HERBAL ICED TEA

VANILLA CUPCAKES WITH
PINK FROSTING

Organic yogurt and fruit

FOR 10 MONTHS AND OLDER

¼ cup plain organic yogurt

¼ cup cooked (steamed), unsweetened organic raspberries (or fruit of choice)

COMBINE the yogurt and fruit, mashing the lumps of fruit for a smoother texture.

the SCENT

Sweet honey and . . . fragrance-free wipes

BABIES ARE KNOWN FOR THEIR SWEET BREATH and scrumptious-smelling skin. They're also known for their frequent and often ill-timed diaper-filling abilities. Entertaining the toddler set involves just a little forethought on this subject, and Racquel and I decided simply to move her adorable white changing table from the nursery to the spacious downstairs bathroom. This way moms and babies could have a convenient and quiet diaper-changing space away from the party. Honey-scented pampering creams and powders were on hand, as well as lots of eco-friendly wipes. By the end of the party, all the little girls were clean, full, and smelling like honey, and all the mommies looked visibly refreshed from the gentle breezes and afternoon sunshine dappling the leaves of the trees.

the SOUND

. . . Ga-ga, goo-goo!

EVEN IF A ONE YEAR-OLD ISN'T LURCHING toward those first steps yet, she's starting to test her language skills at full volume. This is the age for classic "baby talk," and at Chloe's party much of the conversation sounded a little something like this: "Gabal-dee ga-ga blab-bal-dee goop." As every mom knows, young kids can become overstimulated very fast, and the combined excitement of five babies and five mommies was plenty to get these girls "talking" up a storm. My contribution to the sound track was minimal; in fact, I did nothing. Sometimes, however, I do like to bring a basket of instruments to toddler parties. Babies as young as one are old enough to play with a wacky kazoo or a basic bongo. I've also been known to pop a Mozart CD into gift bags at baby parties. Who knows whether classical music can actually make kids smarter, but one thing it can definitely do is make moms a lot calmer — and that's good for the whole family.

- A word of advice about babies and bouquets: flowers are not so great around the little ones. They tend to want to grab the pretty flowers and eat them, and since a surprising number of flowers are poisonous, this can be a problem.

- You can create a virtual boundary to your party space outdoors by using helium balloons. Create clusters of balloon bouquets with beautiful ribbons tied to a brick or rock wrapped in paper or cloth as an anchor and place them around the perimeter of the space.

- Balloons have a shelf life, so you should always prepare them last, allowing for about eight hours until the balloons lose their firmness and start to wilt and fall.

- When popped, rubber balloons become a dangerous choking hazard for babies and toddlers. Keep balloons out of children's reach and make sure to pick up any bits of rubber that may fall to the ground.

- Be picture perfect: always have a camera on hand. Digital cameras are great for instant gratification, and if mom has a portable printer (like one of the HP Photosmart printers, which are perfect because they don't need to be hooked up to a computer) close to the party space, she can enjoy a keepsake even before the party ends.

- A cake blazing with candles can be frightening to small children. Try a less fiery collection of cupcakes instead and save the candles for the years to come. This way, you'll enjoy the photo op but forgo the tears.

- Create a ribbon drawer at home. Save pretty ribbons from gift boxes and bags so that you can reuse them with balloons and gifts in the future. This is a great way to recycle.

- When making homemade baby food, the possibilities are endless, but guard against unexpected allergic reactions by not using any ingredients that your baby hasn't had yet.

- When entertaining outside, consider having a basket of inexpensive flip-flop sandals available so that your guests can kick off their fancy shoes and relax (especially if that might involve playing on the lawn).

- Hire a babysitter or two on the day of your party and have him or her come a few hours early to lend a hand so that you can prepare properly. Each mom will be glad to have an extra set of hands during party time — it might turn out to be the best "favor" of all!

Terrible twos, here we come!

AS ANY PARENT WILL TELL YOU, children grow up fast. One day you're folding a T-shirt the size of your hand and before you know it . . . well, the T-shirt may be the same size, but your daughter will be eighteen and wearing it to a rock concert. That's just one of the reasons it's so important to commemorate the different steps children take along life's path. In some sense, birthday commemorations serve as gifts to parents and children alike, and little party favors that last are a great addition to any first-birthday celebration. At the end of Chloe's party, each little girl smiled broadly as she clutched her very own teddy bear from the place setting, and the mothers smiled just as widely as they clutched the personalized bibs and engraved silver baby bracelets, both reminders of a pleasant outing on a sunny afternoon with their daughters and friends. Still, I think Chloe's mother wore the biggest smile of all when I presented her with the time capsule I had made to hold all the photos and mementos of her daughter's birthday celebrations. For now, there was just one picture in it — a digital photo of Chloe and Racquel playing together on the grass — but there would be many more happy returns to come.

Kevin's 5th

A FATHER-AND-SON FISHING PARTY

for sixteen

Usually when I meet with a client, we sit on couches, sip coffee, and talk about wine pairings and weather contingency plans. However, when I met with Kevin, the cause célèbre of this outdoorsy fifth-birthday party, we sat on the floor, ramming dump trucks into throw cushions for much of the time. While I discussed possible locations with Kevin's parents, I helped Kevin dislodge a toy crane from the jaws of his pet dog. My point is, when it comes to planning a party for kids, I have two clients instead of one, and they don't always have the same ideas about what makes for a good time. Parents want to minimize hassle, prevent accidents, make sure games are fair, hide breakables, and enjoy an easy setup and speedy cleanup. Five-year-olds, on the other hand, want to hang upside down, play make-believe games, eat candy, get presents, and run in circles all day long. It's my job to please both sides — but then, I guess my job is always about finding a balance between hanging the perfect chandeliers and swinging from them!

Of course, once I discovered Kevin's newfound love of fishing trips with Dad and the small lake nestled behind their country home, I forgot about chandeliers altogether. I decided I would thrill both fathers and sons alike by staging a low-fuss lakeside fishing party with something for everyone. Kevin and his gang of friends would enjoy an early fishing lesson that was sure to dance in their minds for years to come, complete with canisters brimming with Gummy Worms, steel buckets loaded with their first sets of fishing gear, and an audience of adoring fathers. At the same time, those adoring fathers would be treated to an adult version of this exciting day: a tranquil "adult habitat" — with a soothing menu of updated campground comfort foods — would promise a temporary retreat into their own memories of nature as their sons explored the waterside under special supervision. Perhaps one day while stuck in a jam-packed car pool lane or standing in line in a crowded grocery store, they, too, would have the pleasure of recalling this first-time fishing expedition with their kids. Without a doubt, this versatile "big birthday" would reel in every single guest — hook, line, and sinker.

Without a doubt, this versatile first "big birthday" would reel in every single guest, hook, line, and sinker.

A cultivated campground

I WANTED THIS WHOLE PARTY to look like it spilled right out of Dad's old fishing tackle. To focus the party space, I decorated the surrounding trees with colorful bobbers. A low table for the pint-size half of the party featured lots of tall glass canisters filled with Swedish Fish candy, toy frogs that "hopped" around the place settings, and an endless supply of worms — Gummy Worms, that is. Some of the canisters were accented with a little ribbon around the edge (attached with hot glue) and decorated with little plastic frogs set on top, while others were filled with water, blue marbles, and a colorful glass fish. A fun fish-printed tablecloth covered the surface for easy cleanup. Tin mugs and matching plates took the question of breakables out of the party altogether but not without adding a little campfire chic. Red bandanas were the Boy Scout equivalent of fine linen napkins.

A classic wicker fishing tackle dangling from the back of each stool looked good enough to appear on the New York fashion scene — think Great Lakes à la Ralph Lauren — but for the time being, it held all the necessary tools for the children to hit the pond with their rods and reels.

It also served as the perfect party favor, reminding the children of the exciting day they spent learning to fish. A galvanized steel bucket decorated with paper fish and filled with a fishing hat, candy, and still more fishing gear also did double duty: as another party favor for the kids to take home and as a tribute to the minimalist aesthetics of a well-spent day at the docks.

What about my other, less candy-fueled clients, you ask? The fathers' table also featured a boyish campground, with blue bandana napkins, more tin mugs, and a simple denim tablecloth. But with a keen awareness that nature lovers of all ages love totally different things about nature, I splurged on an imaginative bird-sanctuary "tablescape" that brought the soothing charms of the woods to the center of the party. Using moss-covered Oasis floral foam and small stones as a base, I arranged a series of hand-carved wooden birds down the center of the table to evoke the idea of a teeming nature reserve. Tall ornamental grasses matched to the indigenous flora of the area spiked upward for a dramatic habitat re-creation that made the fathers in search of a relaxing afternoon in the forest feel equally at home.

Bird-sanctuary runner

However you arrange this "organic" centerpiece, have fun with it. You can't mess it up!

MATERIALS

- 8 bricks Oasis floral foam
- 8 plastic trays to hold the Oasis
- ornamental cut grasses of different heights and textures (some of my favorites are plume grass, feather reed grass, Japanese silver grass, fountain grass, and purple moor grass)
- sheet moss
- river rocks
- hand-carved wooden birds

METHOD

1. Soak the Oasis in water until it is completely saturated.

2. In order to keep the tablecloth clean and dry, place plastic trays down the length of the table. Fill them with the water-soaked Oasis.

3. Cluster the cut grasses and arrange them in the Oasis by pushing them firmly through to the bottom.

4. Cover the Oasis and the plastic trays with sheet moss to mask them completely.

5. Accent the display with river rocks and wooden birds.

Yes, you can touch

CALL IT A SLIGHT to the honorary mascot if you will, but the textures of this lakeside party were decidedly unscaly. In fact, the overall feel of this gathering was smooth and weather-beaten, like a favorite canvas fishing hat or an old pair of Docksides. Moss and reedy grasses in the centerpiece and worn wicker fishing tackles created a rough-hewn-rowboat feel. Every item on the table, from the tin mugs to the bandana napkins, evoked a rustic fishing trip, just without the fish. And perhaps even more important, every item on the table had to be tough and durable for the children to play with. Put yourself in the shoes of a child: what could be more un-birthdaylike than a party where you can't touch anything? One of the best things about an outdoor party built entirely from scratch to endure all the elements — even children — is that it's easy to keep track of any safety hazards that might prove tempting to a child. For instance, all the hooks on the fishing rods at this party stayed strictly in adult hands. That gave the afternoon the perfect laid-back feel for all the future anglers and their parents.

Grilled cheese, my favorite!

EVERY TIME I NOTICE a hip "comfort food" restaurant opening up in Manhattan, I am reminded that the foods we love most as kids are often the foods we love most forever. That's why catering for children and adults at the same time is not as difficult as it sounds. Much like fishing, some things never go out of style. For Kevin's father-and-son fifth birthday I recalled my camping trips from years past and rolled out the mother of all outdoor comfort foods: soup and sandwiches. At the children's table some well-placed goldfish crackers made tomato soup taste like a boatload of fun, while the dads enjoyed a slightly upscale soup — steaming bowls of hearty clam chowder with croutons.

The remainder of the meal paid even greater tribute to what the two tables would always have in common. Young and old alike dug into crispy, melt-in-your-mouth grilled cheese sandwiches, and the adults looked just as excited as the kids when the fanciful fishing tackle–themed sculpted cheesecake from elegantcheesecakes.com arrived all aglow with candles. The children's sandwiches were cut into fish shapes with a simple cookie cutter, and the dads' sandwiches were made with a robust loaf of rustic bread, Gruyère cheese, and mayonnaise. The children put a lot more thought than the dads into who got which piece of tackle as the cheesecake was divided among them. When all is said and done, the earliest birthdays we celebrate create lasting memories through our most basic senses, and on that crisp October afternoon, I saw that happening: at the same time, both Kevin and his father looked up from their empty plates and said, "Yum!"

the Menu

EASY OVEN-GRILLED CHEESE FOR KIDS AND ADULTS

CLAM CHOWDER FOR THE ADULTS

TOMATO SOUP...JAZZED UP FOR THE KIDS

CREEL CHEESECAKE

Easy oven-grilled cheese

I'VE NICKNAMED THESE "ROCK SANDWICHES"

8 slices bread

4 slices American cheese

1 stick melted butter

1 tablespoon dried thyme

fish-shaped cookie cutter

PREHEAT the oven to 400 degrees.

CUT each slice of bread using the cookie cutter. Do the same with each slice of cheese.

IN a small bowl, mix the melted butter and dried thyme. Using a pastry brush, lightly brush the inside of each piece of bread with the butter and start assembling your sandwiches.

BRUSH the outside of both sides of the sandwich with more melted butter.

PLACE the assembled sandwiches on a nonstick baking sheet and place them in the oven.

BAKE for 8 to 10 minutes, until golden brown.

FOR THE ADULTS

8 slices sourdough bread

1/2 cup mayonnaise

3 tablespoons finely chopped sun-dried tomatoes

1 teaspoon freshly ground pepper

1/2 teaspoon ground mustard seed

4 slices Gruyère cheese

2 tablespoons melted butter

PREHEAT the oven to 400 degrees.

IN a small bowl mix the mayonnaise, sun-dried tomatoes, pepper, and mustard seed until well combined. Spread a thin layer of the mixture on the inside of two slices of bread. Add a slice of cheese and assemble the sandwich. Brush the outside of both sides of the sandwich with melted butter.

PLACE the assembled sandwiches on a nonstick baking sheet and place them in the oven.

BAKE for 8 to 10 minutes, until golden brown.

Tomato soup . . . jazzed up

4 cups prepared tomato soup (fresh or canned)

1/2 cup Italian bread crumbs

1/4 cup finely chopped fresh basil

1/4 cup heavy cream

salt and pepper to taste

Goldfish crackers, for garnish

PREPARE the soup according to the directions. Add the bread crumbs, basil, cream, salt, and pepper, stirring occasionally.

SERVE WARM. Garnish with Goldfish crackers.

the SCENT

Don't forget the "nose buds"

SCENT IS ONE AREA where the aspects of a real-life fishing trip do *not* need to be re-created or amplified. Of course, this is not to say the "nose buds" should be ignored. Whenever you entertain outdoors, make sure to do a quick "smell check." When I sniff out a great location, sometimes I am literally sniffing it! Occasionally there is a fishy odor near a pond or dock, or, in the country, there might be a breeze blowing in from a nearby stable. If this is the case, reconsider the dining location, or, if the odor is very mild, keep the grills stoked with charcoal, the citronella burning, and a few fragrant leaves or flowers on or around the table. For this distinctly nonfloral and child-centric party, I relied on eucalyptus branches and pine needles to freshen the air without overwhelming the little fishermen with the kind of perfumes deemed improper at such boyhood rituals. Though there were no fishy smells in Kevin's backyard, these little aromatic touches were so subtle that we could all pay more attention to the mouth-watering aroma of grilled cheese sandwiches on the broiler!

Dust off the campfire songbook

FIVE-YEAR-OLDS LOVE A GOOD SING-ALONG. If one of the attending dads enjoys playing guitar, consider a sing-along after dinner (but before dessert — otherwise the kids may be too hyper for a round of "Row, Row, Row Your Boat"). This is how Kevin's father brought a rousing sound to this long afternoon, one that both his son's friends and his own buddies could appreciate together. As far as I'm concerned, this is the most interactive way to liven up the events of the day for all involved. Small children tend to compete with loud recordings by yelling, which can make for a deafening experience. And stereo tunes almost never offer the same memories as running through a campfire songbook. Still, Kevin's party convinced me that at the proper juncture a little background music in the great outdoors can be just the ticket, especially for bringing down the energy level of all those tiny partygoers. After the fishing was done, the meal was over, and the birthday cake was served, a mix of child-friendly music from reggae to rockabilly floated softly on the breeze for a festive third-act wind-down. As the children's dancing slowed and eyelids began to droop, the parents stayed to hear one last song.

TUTERA tips

○ When entertaining young kids and parents, set a "kids' table" next to or near the "grown-ups' table." This gives the children a little independence while keeping them at arm's length.

○ Whenever a child's party takes place in or around water (pond, lake, pool, etc.), make sure to have life jackets on hand. Safety must always come first!

○ Insect repellent is essential when you're entertaining outside — especially near water, where mosquitoes like to linger. For easy access and application, display the repellent on a small table.

○ Keep in mind that children's attention spans can run short. Plan enough activities to keep them happy but not so many that they become overwhelmed.

○ Remember to make food fun for kids. Try using cookie cutters to transform sandwich bread into unique shapes and sizes. For Kevin's party, we cut sandwiches into the shape of fish. Have some fun creating shapes that match your party's theme. You can use snowflakes for winter or holiday parties, hearts for Valentine's Day, or flower shapes for a girls' afternoon tea.

○ If you have a pond on your property, install a floating fountain — it will keep your pond and fish healthier.

○ Take advantage of your natural surroundings and offer outdoor activities such as playing with remote-control boats or planes, taking pony rides, going on interactive scavenger hunts, or flying kites. A kids' party can be educational, too. Teach your guests how to do something new, such as feed fish or protect the environment. You could also do some bird-watching or make a variety of birdhouses.

○ You don't have to use conventional chairs for a party. Small stools, ottomans, and crates work well, too. Bales of hay are terrific for a country-and-western-style party. Cover the hay with blankets to make it more comfy to sit on.

○ It's great to use a few elements from your surrounding environment as decor on the table. Try grasses, stones, branches, rocks, and wildflowers. Rinse your natural "ornaments" with a little water first to remove dirt and prevent small bugs from creeping onto the table.

○ Small coffee mugs (metal or plastic) are perfect for serving soup to kids. The size is right and the handle makes for easy lifting. Take a quick trip to a camping supply store (online or in person) to find some you like.

To catch a . . . fish!

OF COURSE, poor little Kevin didn't actually catch any fish at his birthday party. Apparently he was so excited to help all of his friends learn to cast their lines that he completely forgot to watch his own! A couple of his friends managed to reel in some lake trout, and after some discussion and bravado ("It's a two footer!" screamed one boy with a vivid imagination), they tossed one after another back where they came from. Even though Kevin and his friends seemed almost as excited about the Swedish Fish and the Gummy Worms as they were about the real deal, it was clear that the day would be meaningful for years to come. Kevin's dad beamed as he told me that the next morning, his son woke him early with the brightest of eyes and an eager request. Less than an hour later, the two had rowed out into the middle of the lake with a thermos of leftover soup, Kevin's new fishing tackle, and only the refrain of "Row, Row, Row Your Boat" to guide them through the misty waters.

Lucy's Sweet 16th

A "PRETTY IN PINK" EVENING

for thirty-five

I always think of the sweet sixteen party as one of the great lost rituals in American culture. There was a time when it seemed like every girl in the country was issued a birth certificate, a pair of pink booties, and her own giddy vision of this classic milestone party. Needless to say, a lot has changed since then — most sixteen-year-olds today already have elaborate career strategies to think about, and their giddy visions do not include escort cards and custom centerpieces. But that's no reason to abandon one of the most gratifying birthday rituals of the teenage years.

That's why I was so thrilled to meet Lucy, an aspiring young fashion designer with a totally contemporary sense of ambition but a true appreciation for the pleasures of old-school ceremony, too. Talk about a girl after my own heart! When she and her mother asked me to dream up a sweet sixteen bash that went "the whole nine yards," I jumped at the chance to reinvent this classic birthday event for the twenty-first-century girl, and I already had a plan in mind. Lucy's super-smart hot pink ensemble screamed the only two words I needed to hear: *Glam Girl.* Using her designs for inspiration, I planned a formal soirée — complete with escort cards — that blended Lucy's passionate dreams of a future career in fashion with the fun-loving whimsy only sixteen-year-olds can honestly claim for their own. Re-creations of her funky fashion ideas — which full-scale mannequin bodices and drawings trimmed with purple and pink fabrics brought vividly to life — would offer friends and family an opportunity to wander through the pages of Lucy's sketchbook. Bright gerbera daisies and darling rosebuds, combined with loads more solid pink and purple fabrics, outrageous feather boas, and vintage handbags, brooches, and high heels, would dress up every table with a fashion-forward sense of teen spirit. And best of all, the whole thing would take place in New York City during the world-famous Fashion Week at Bryant Park, so Lucy and her friends would enjoy an exclusive glimpse at some real-deal fanfare. Like Chanel's timeless "little black dress," this sweet sixteen would win rave reviews from the edgiest critics in town: tomorrow's fashion tycoons.

There was a time when it seemed like every girl in the country was issued a birth certificate, a pair of pink booties, and her own giddy vision of this classic milestone party.

Glam girl

MY DESIGN CONCEPT FOR THE PARTY (and the clothes) reflected Lucy's own eclectic style: funky downtown glam meets fabulous uptown chic. By mixing hipster essentials (sequins, berets, halter tops, and "bling bling" shimmer) with swanky couture style (big hair, black-tie chiffon, and matching purses), I created an edgy and energetic design perfect for the modern debutante. The color scheme needed to vibrate: I opted for hot new-wave pink and deep disco purple.

The location, Divine Studio in New York City, was haunted by the ghosts of fabulous fashion shoots. This spare white loft space has been the backdrop for photographs appearing in *Vogue, Allure, Glamour,* and just about every other fashion magazine out there. The guests could feel like supermodels for a day, since we suggested on the invitation that they dress up "Glam Girl" style. Once the loft was filled with the girls (and their fashion statements), it was as if Fashion Week had spilled over from Bryant Park right into the party.

Each element of the decor paid homage to the designer's "process": I created life-size fashion sketches on foam board and decorated them with swatches, draped fabric, and the odd splash of color. These were positioned

Glam girl sketch

MATERIALS

○ clear transparency

○ projector

○ 4 x 8-foot white foam core (at least ½ inch thick)

○ black marker and colored markers

○ scrap fabric, cut into pieces

○ fashion magazine

METHOD

1. Trace a picture from the fashion magazine or draw a sketch onto the clear transparency.

2. Use a projector to enlarge the image on the foam core to the desired size.

3. Outline the image on the foam core with a black marker. Color it in or shade it.

4. Add pieces of fabric as desired to accent.

5. Prop the images up against the walls.

around the room to help hem in the expansive loft space a little and add some color to the white background. Each sketch featured a different personal style to correspond with Lucy's greatest fashion inspirations (her glam girlfriends, of course).

Mannequins fitted with custom creations (à la Couture Tutera) became the focal point for the table centerpieces. Surrounding the mannequins were feather boas, gerbera daisies, and roses spilling upward from flea-market shoes and handbags — a girl's ultimate accessories — adding a groovy vintage feel to the scene.

Each table was decked out in one color (a variation on the pink and purple theme), with matching napkins and flowers. Napkin rings were made from small pieces of a marabou feather boa and accented with costume jewelry pins. Surrounding chairs were "dressed" to match, with chair backs custom-made to look like little cocktail dresses. Glam Girl plates and glassware put a bit of sass into each setting, and sparkling coin purses served as place-card holders as well as party favors. The escort-card table was a beautiful "mess" of toppled hatboxes and tangled feather boas; it appeared to have been recently hit by a storm of frantic models. Nestled into this glamorous chaos were small escort cards dangling on miniature hangers.

Chilled strawberry soup

3 cups fresh strawberries, hulled

2 quarts vanilla ice cream, softened

¾ cup heavy cream

2 tablespoons lime juice

lavender-colored sugar

COMBINE all the ingredients except the sugar in a large bowl. Transfer the mixture into a food processor in small batches and process until it is almost smooth. Ladle the soup into individual goblets rimmed with lavender-colored sugar (this is easily done by rubbing the edge of the goblet with a lemon wedge and then dipping it into a plate filled with sugar). Serve chilled. Garnish with a sliced strawberry (optional).

Pink or purple mock-tail sparkler

2 ounces pink lemonade (for pink) or grape juice (for purple)

splash of white cranberry juice

chilled sparkling cider

raspberry or blackberry, for garnish

PLACE ice in a highball glass. Add the lemonade (or grape juice) and cranberry juice. Top it with chilled cider and garnish with a raspberry or blackberry.

the SCENT

Sugar and spice and all things nice

THEY SAY GIRLS ARE MADE OF SUGAR AND SPICE. Well, it sure isn't science, but it sets a wonderfully fragrant tone for a sweet sixteen party that mixes the hip and the fun, the retro and the contempo — or, to take a little inspiration from Britney Spears, the girl and the woman. I planned Lucy's tailor-made evening so that every sensation her guests experienced would blend perfectly with the larger design for the space. After all, you can tell whether any design is a good one — on the runway or at a party — by how well it awakens your various senses. Here, the sweet floral scent of the roses in each centerpiece bloomed with unadorned cheer. The natural fruit essences that punched up the menu, from fresh strawberries to rich mangoes, suffused the air with an organic aroma as invigorating as it was comforting. But it was the subtle perfume of lavender and the energizing essence of mint that put a grown-up herbal finish on the mix, blending a hint of aromatherapy with the fabled sweetness of girlhood.

the SOUND

Vogue!

PUMPING DANCE TRACKS ARE DE RIGUEUR on the catwalk. The fashion industry must have scientific proof that even the plainest clothes when accompanied by a George Michael remix just look better. Suffice it to say, there was some crossover between a typical Bryant Park Fashion Week sound track and Lucy's own iPod playlist: every hot club mix and techno track was in rotation. I was amused to discover that many of Lucy's "new" favorite songs were the same as many of my "old," and very familiar, favorite songs from the eighties. While Lucy sent me cruising down memory lane with Culture Club and Cyndi Lauper, I sent her to new heights of eighties pop passion by introducing her to vintage Madonna and Prince. New technology makes it possible to program music digitally, leaving you with the job of kitting out the space with adequate speakers and amplifiers. When setting up your own music mixes for a party, always test the technology (CDs, MP3 player, speakers, etc.) beforehand. The last thing you want to deal with on the night of the party is a missing speaker cable or a cranky CD player and a frantic trip to the nearest RadioShack. For Lucy's party we opted for a professional female DJ. Her *nom de glam* was "Star 80." When she showed up in Dolce-this and Gucci-that, she sent the girls into absolute fits of admiration. Once Madonna's "Vogue" remix started pumping, they all ditched their nonalcoholic champagne and hit the dance floor.

TUTERA tips

○ Instead of poking candle holes in an especially exquisite cake, use small candleholders around the base of the cake instead. You get the same glowing effect without touching the precious cake. Sturdy rose heads cut flush at the base with a candle pushed into the center work beautifully.

○ A blank party space (such as a photographer's loft) allows for any decorating option imaginable, but it's not always best for the budget-conscious — even a minimalist approach can get costly. A great way to create a fabulous look without spending a lot is to select one or two colors and use them in abundance. One color, or one decorative item, used en masse can achieve a big WOW in any room.

○ If you can't decide on just one color for the decor of your party, select two complementary colors and create alternating monochromatic table settings throughout the room. This ensures a bold and dramatic effect.

○ Try using inexpensive (and unusual) containers in place of vases. The handbags and shoes used for Lucy's party were all flea market finds for under $5 each.

○ Parents rarely know much about what their teenager listens to. So ask your teenager to pick out CDs or have her or him speak to the DJ before the party. Remind both of them to add variety to the style and mood of the music to help shift the energy of the party throughout the night. It's also important to give the DJ a list of "don't plays."

○ When celebrating a teenager's birthday, consider having a daytime party for the family and an evening party for the friends. This way everyone is happy, and there is no danger of the adults taking over the teenager's "space."

○ Fashionable clothes are not just for wearing. You can create fun chair backs by "dressing" the back of an ordinary rental chair in a cute outfit to match the theme of the party (I've done this with tuxedos, gowns, cocktail dresses, and more). Take a trip to a fabric store and ask for leftover goods they are not selling. All you need is a yard or two per chair and a household stapler. Pins, feathers, and beads are useful accessories.

○ Use a digital camera to take photographs at your party (just like the paparazzi!) and have a portable printer at a side table to print the images and hand them out to guests before they leave. It's a great way to give them an instant memory.

○ To provide an interactive activity for your guests, create a self-serve "cake station." Have your caterer or baker make a simple white cake and set up a station full of fun toppings, from fudge and strawberries to M&M's (in the color scheme of your party) and ice cream. Your guests will have a ball creating their own custom confections.

○ To mix up the ordinary flow of a birthday party, sing "Happy Birthday" and serve the cake as the first course. It will surprise your guests and be a fun way to start the party.

A runway success

SEEING LUCY AND HER FRIENDS savor every minute of her big night only confirmed my belief in holding on to some version of the traditional sweet sixteen celebration. For one special night, they had a chance to see themselves as the sophisticated adults they would soon become and to take themselves and their dreams of glamour seriously but with the perfect zeal that comes strictly with youth. With equal measures of gravity and glee, each one clutched the snazzy little coin purse that served first as a place-card holder and then as a fun souvenir of the night's festivities. At the end of the night I could only smile as they all danced and sang along to Cyndi Lauper's classic "Girls Just Want to Have Fun" with clear commitment to that age-old pursuit. Cyndi only got it about half right — girls want fun and so much more — but for that glorious chorus, together they had it all.

Dylan's 25th
A DISCO INFERNO
for a group of twenty-somethings

Whether the topic concerns political parties or soft drink preferences, there are few things every person agrees on. In fact, there might be only one: turning twenty-five marks the occasion for a serious party. Twenty-five is the turning point toward adulthood for most twenty-somethings. It's a symbolic time to throw a wild celebration that resembles the past years of crazy nights out, before moving on to a different type of commemoration. There is, of course, much less agreement about what makes a party serious—some dream of a raucous maiden voyage to a local dive bar, while others envision a formal affair with family members and professional photographers. The most important thing from my perspective, though, is to make the honoree of every twenty-fifth birthday party I throw feel the thrill of standing on the cusp of something big, outrageous, and just for them—call it a New Year's Eve of the self.

It was thrilling. I took this concept to its limit while planning a twenty-fifth bash for a friend's son. An aspiring artist and a big fan of Andy Warhol's pop art, Dylan wore the look of a guy who'd already seen everything, taken a picture, and sold a thousand T-shirts bearing its print. I knew I would have to think big to wow him, so I set out to reinvent the storied parties of clubs like Studio 54 (which he knew only from the movies) for a smarter, slicker age. Once I got a glimpse of Dylan's artwork in his Alphabet City loft, I knew color and motion would be very important. With its high ceilings, multiple levels, and dark walls, New York's famous Crobar Club served as the perfect canvas for a dynamic birthday spectacle built around Dylan's energetic creative spirit and wry sense of humor. The pop art decor would literally rain down from the ceiling: bright red and orange umbrellas kissed with crystal raindrops would hang in midair alongside sweeping colored banners that would float like giant brushstrokes, with still more umbrellas blooming like flowers from a vase. Sleek Lucite boxes in bold solid colors and funky Plexiglas candelabras would dress up tables big enough for crowds of friends, while repurposed products like Post-it Notes and Brillo pads would add design elements witty enough for clever, postmodern sensibilities. But what about that crucial wow factor? Have no fear. To put a glamorous, lighthearted spin on the evening's festivities, I launched Flutter Fetti cannons filled with colorful confetti to shower on the entire entourage at midnight sharp, just when the clock signaled the first hour of his official birthday. It would be Dylan's night to feel like a bona fide star, but somewhere up there, in that great discotheque in the sky, I knew Warhol would be celebrating this off-kilter New Year as his own, too.

> The most important thing is to make the honoree of every twenty-fifth birthday party feel the thrill of standing on the cusp of something big, outrageous, and just for them.

Pop goes the confetti

WHEN ANDY WARHOL ONCE FILLED AN ART GALLERY with nothing but huge silver balloons, he was onto something. Art isn't just for the walls. It can literally bounce from ceiling to floor and back again. And that was exactly the inspiration behind the decor for Dylan's wildly downtown and superkinetic twenty-fifth. Bright orange and red umbrellas did not just pop up from the tables, they dangled in midair as if suspended magically in a gravity-free zone, and they came bursting up and out from the sides of the room like daisies reaching for the sunshine. After all, when entertaining in a space with high ceilings, it is always important to remember that the air itself is a part of your canvas. With this in mind I added long strands of invisible thread holding tiny crystal raindrops — as if frozen midway to the ground — among the umbrellas. I hung long, billowing swatches of sheer red, purple, and yellow materials from the rafters so that the disco lights would stream through them, casting rainbows of color over the dancing guests below.

HOW to Painted votive candles and plates

MATERIALS

o glass votive candle holders, plates, martini glasses, etc.

o glass paint (or glass paint pens)

o acrylic paint

o small synthetic paintbrush

METHOD

1. Using acrylic and glass paint and a synthetic brush, paint the glass with whatever designs you like. Don't paint the top two inches of the glass. If you're painting plates, do only the bottom side. You can cover the votive holders completely.

2. Allow them to dry.

To continue my 3-D effects, I created surreal centerpieces that literally rose up out of long rectangular tables almost as if they were a part of an elaborate stage show. Bronzed mannequin hands seemed to be propping up bronze votive holders, while a jumble of clear and angular martini glasses toppled to either side. Beneath the rising bronze light show was a shallow pool of water filled with exotic flowers and floating candles in bobbing glass candleholders. Cocktail tables featured purple pillar candles sheathed in unrolled Brillo pads, and small yellow candles around simple lamps in Post-it Note shades. (These are *so* easy to make and provide lots of interaction potential: "Can I get your number?" was never easier.) I also placed a few pop bouquets of dried paintbrushes in square glass vases on the cocktail tables. An additional and longer table featured orange and purple Plexiglas boxes illuminated by votives in purple-painted holders, as well as two surreal Plexiglas candelabras. The colorful boxes were not empty, either; upon close inspection, guests found floating rubber duckies or stacks of light bulbs inside them. All of the tables were dressed in downtown black with tops made from Xeroxed cereal box covers and covered with clear vinyl. Once the Flutter Fetti filled the air from above, the room itself seemed to be dancing!

HOW to Spin-art invitation

MATERIALS

- ○ pinking shears
- ○ white card stock
- ○ acrylic craft paint (3 or 4 different colors)
- ○ vellum paper
- ○ salad spinner
- ○ hole punch
- ○ ribbon
- ○ large square envelopes

METHOD

1. Using pinking shears, cut the card stock into three different-size circles. The largest one should be no bigger than the bottom of your salad spinner, the next one about an inch smaller, and the last one, one inch smaller than the second.

2. Place one round card in the bottom of your salad spinner and drop a few dots of paint in the center. Close the lid on the spinner and turn the spinner several times. Add more paint (in different colors each time) until you have achieved a nice layering of color. Carefully remove the card and set it aside to dry. Repeat for each card.

3. Print the invitation information on the vellum paper with your home computer. Using pinking shears, cut the vellum so that it's a little smaller than the round cards. (You can use two layers of vellum if necessary to fit the information.)

4. Place the vellum and the three cards together and punch a hole in the top. Thread a small ribbon through the opening and tie it.

5. Mail the invitation in a large square envelope.

NOTE: Be sure to check with your local post office for correct postage.

Unbreakable!

I ALWAYS LET MY IMAGINATION TAKE THE LEAD when it comes to decorating a party space — let's call it "right-brain party planning." Creativity reigns supreme. Once the ideas have been generated, however, it's time for the left brain to take over and for the fantasy to be realized in practical, logical terms. This is when a sculpture of toppling martini glasses becomes a sculpture of toppling *Plexiglas* martini glasses, and this is when a crystal candelabra becomes a *plastic* candleholder with a fancy candelabra etched on it. When drinks are going to slide across bar tops or get hastily planted on the nearest table the minute the right beat takes hold, it's a good idea to leave the fragile china and glassware back in the armoire at home. Of course, the actual cocktails deserve the best possible treatment, and at Dylan's party they were served in stylish shot glasses and groovy tumblers. This party was all about rubber, plastic, paper, and nylon, and everything had a glossy and fabulous sheen of the artificial. Just as the pop artists of the sixties embraced a new wave of man-made materials, so did I. Plexiglas boxes held rubber duckies, while nylon umbrellas exploded from PVC containers. Plastic mannequin hands spray-painted bronze took on a metallic glow. Tabletops were covered in glossy paper, and the chairs were plastic, which, strangely enough, made the perfect setting for a night of excitement that was most definitely the real thing.

Snack to your art's content

THE BEST POP ART is fun but provocative; outlandish but familiar; curious but utterly appealing. That's a tall order to begin with, but when you plan to eat your pop art, it has to be more than that; it has to be plain old delicious, too. Despite these challenges, the fabulous chefs at New York's Aroma Kitchen had no problem concocting an eclectic menu of arty hors d'oeuvres that boasted all of these qualities and more for Dylan's birthday blowout. Taking a breather between dance tracks never tasted so good as guests munched on a smorgasbord of soup shots, gourmet pizzas, and cones filled with intriguing surprises. Fresh, bursting flavors, wildly colorful ingredients, and exciting combinations made every bite feel like savoring a hot remix that trumps even the original. The asparagus soup with a sporty spear of its star ingredient and a luxurious hint of caviar and lemon cream was cool, and not just in temperature; the silky vegetal base and the caviar brine in tart lemon introduced an altogether original palette of flavors. In the true spirit of minimalism, the chilled grape soup with a fun-filled grape swizzle proved that candy-sweet playfulness is an aesthetic, too, and not just for children.

Meanwhile, the tiny pizzas with giant flavor and a striking look could not have been more enticing. Individual pies topped with such delicacies as smoky Washington forest mushrooms, creamy fontina cheese, preserved lemon, and the zest of Italian parsley reinvented old-school party food for a smart new set. And for those who didn't stop dancing to grab a plate, the taste of

the Menu

SOUPS

CHILLED ASPARAGUS WITH CAVIAR, LEMON CREAM, AND SEA SALT

CHILLED GRAPE WITH GRAPE SWIZZLE

CIPOLLINE "ACQUA PAZZA" WITH MUSTARD OIL, THYME, AND LAUREL

MAINE LOBSTER BRODO

PIZZAS

SAFFRON, ARTICHOKE, AND MAINE SHRIMP

RED PEPPER, BASIL PESTO, WALNUT, AND PROVOLONE

WASHINGTON FOREST MUSHROOMS, FONTINA, PRESERVED LEMON, AND PARSLEY

WILD ARUGULA, OLIVES, AND ORGANIC MUSTARD SEED OIL

CONES

SPICY CRAB SALAD WITH VANILLA AND POPPY SEEDS

COCKTAILS

PURPLE PRINCE

CARROT ZING

RED RAIN

LUNAR LEMON QUENCHER

FUNKY ART CHOCOLATE CAKE

the cones filled with spicy crab salad with smooth vanilla and crunchy poppy seeds danced on the tongue right along with them. With standout flavors and style to match, these clever little dishes almost looked too good to eat.

But since the food at Dylan's party had to match the grand scale of the rest of this pop art bonanza, the small bites were just the beginning. When folks got thirsty, they enjoyed one of four irresistible reinventions of the old ho-hum cocktail. Carrot Zing was graced by an outsize disk of melon and a baby carrot, Red Rain was garnished with a frayed Pull-n-Peel Twizzler, and Purple Prince brought every kid's favorite accessory — the Blow Pop — up to date for a new age. There was even a fun-filled frozen cocktail, a Lunar Lemon Quencher. Each drink played a note in the chorus of orange, red, and purple that filled the room with energy and excitement — and made a tasty work of art from a treasured piece of Americana; consider it Dada in a glass. The cake, however, was the superstar of this chic, madcap entourage. Made just for Dylan's party by the incomparable Cheryl Kleinman Cakes, it put the final flourish on an evening filled with witty, delicious spectacles. Brimming with the flavors of chocolate, coconut, and almond, this tribute to the Almond Joy candy bar we all know and love dazzled all with a toppling tower of purple, orange, and red layers that Dr. Seuss himself might have imagined. With each tier covered in madly burning sparklers, it was altogether clear that this particular taste of pop-cultural redux was a true original.

Purple prince

2 ounces vodka

1/2 ounce parfait amour

1 ounce white cranberry juice

1/2 ounce fresh-squeezed lime juice

lemon-lime club soda

Blow Pop, for garnish

INTO a highball glass with ice, pour vodka, parfait amour, white cranberry juice, and lime juice. Stir well. Top with chilled club soda and drop a Blow Pop in (stick side down) for a garnish.

Carrot zing

2 ounces citrus rum

2 ounces carrot-orange-apricot juice (available as a mixture at gourmet stores)

splash of fresh lime juice

club soda

baby carrot and horned melon (Kiwaño), for garnish

INTO a highball glass with ice, pour the rum and juices. Stir well and top with chilled club soda. Stir again and garnish with a baby carrot with stalk and a slice of horned melon.

Red rain

2 ounces gin

2 ounces guava juice

1 ounce passion fruit juice

1/2 ounce lime juice

1/2 ounce grenadine

club soda

strawberry Pull-n-Peel Twizzler, as garnish

INTO a highball glass with ice, pour the gin, juices, and grenadine. Stir well and top with chilled club soda. Garnish with a frayed red Pull-n-Peel Twizzler.

Lunar lemon quencher

SERVES 5

1 cup bottled margarita mix

1/2 cup rum

6 ounces Minute Maid® Lemonade

5 cups ice

lemon slices, for garnish

BLEND together the margarita mix, lemonade, and rum.

ADD ice and blend for 45 to 60 seconds or until well mixed.

GARNISH with lemon slices.

the SCENT

Keep it clean

I LOVE GOING TO DANCE CLUBS. But if you ever set foot in one during the light of day, you will undoubtedly be greeted with the lingering aroma of *yesterday's* parties. If this is the case and you are expecting to feed your guests, you may need to pay a little extra attention to smell control. Lots of fragrant candles will often do the trick. Make sure they are replenished as the night goes on and that they are kept away from any flammable material. Sometimes I recommend a quick pre-party spray-down of the space. You can buy room fresheners at the grocery store or go for up-market alternatives at the nearest aromatherapy boutique. For Dylan's party we used a bottle of citrus room freshener. Sandalwood and cedar are nice masculine alternatives. These bottled fragrances do wonders for musty clubs, stale barns, or moldy outdoor tented spaces. Of course, nothing smells quite so perfect as hot wood oven–baked pizzas. Once those little beauties came out of the kitchen, Dylan's twenty-fifth smelled as good as it looked.

the SOUND

Keep the energy mounting

ONE ASSUMPTION I come across frequently is that all a dance party requires, in terms of music, is a seemingly endless supply of dance tracks. Granted, the dance music does carry the night at a certain point, but the whole night should not be dominated by the pounding bass of a techno backbeat. If your venue or club provides an in-house DJ for a reasonable price, I say go for it. But be sure to sit down and discuss *your* style of music first. And make sure the mood of the music changes throughout the night.

Dylan worked with his DJ to select a lot of arty rock music to start off the night, with songs like the Velvet Underground's "Take a Walk on the Wild Side" and the Doors' "Light My Fire" to set a decidedly cool tone. Next came some hits from seventies icons like Blondie and Iggy Pop, and with them came a wave of new energy. Closer to midnight the Studio 54 disco classics kicked in and everyone hit the dance floor. And just as I'd hoped, Dylan was at the center of it all, whirling around in his private disco paradise.

TUTERA tips

- If you want to throw a party in a club, look into clubs that have private rooms or VIP areas that you can rent on regular nights, or see if you can have your party on a night when the club is normally closed.

- When throwing a young, fun party, use one unusual element in abundance to create a dramatic effect (plus, you can get a discount when you buy in bulk). For Dylan's party we opted for umbrellas.

- Confetti isn't what it used to be! You can get hand-operated or automatic Flutter Fetti "cannons." What's more, Flutter Fetti comes in many colors and it's flameproof.

- If you have trouble deciding on one flavor of filling and cake to serve, let each layer be a different flavor with a different filling. Once the cake is sliced and on plates, guests can pick their favorite.

- If your venue/club provides an in-house DJ for a reasonable price, go for it. But be sure to sit down and talk about various styles of music. A variety should be played throughout the night.

- If you want to bring in your own DJ, find out if the club will allow him to tie into the club's sound system. If not, your DJ will need to provide his own.

- It's always a good idea when hosting a party — especially a late-night club party — to have a list of local car services and taxis handy so that your guests can get home safely.

- For a quick way to clean copper if you don't have a specialty cleaner on hand, rub half a lemon and salt on the copper. Another trick is to cover the copper with ketchup, let it sit for a few minutes, and then wipe it off.

- We made columns using foam core and glued colorful plastic plates to them to add a bit of funky color. Be sure to specify the color and thickness when buying foam core (available at your local craft store). You want to make sure you purchase the appropriate kind for sturdiness or flexibility, depending on its use.

- Lighting is a key element when you're throwing a party. It truly brings the party to life!

A blizzard of confetti

WHEN THE CLOCK STRUCK MIDNIGHT and a blizzard of multicolored confetti fell past all the umbrellas and rubber duckies to land on Dylan and his guests, the look of ecstatic surprise on his face said it all. Wow! That look lingered as a local avant-garde performance troupe made up of his friends put the Lite Brite stage I had constructed to good use with an amazing show. Later on, Dylan asked if he could incorporate some of the umbrella sculptures we had built into a living sculpture that would evolve in his studio, and I must say I enjoyed being called "a true party *artiste*." But the most important thing was that for a brief moment Dylan felt like a star and an inspired artist. When the lights went back down and the music came back up, the room swelled with a rainbow of colors, sound, and three-dimensional volume that kept him dancing all night long.

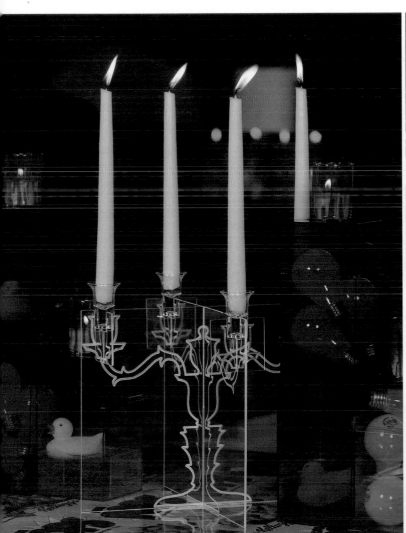

Please join us for a
Black and White Barbecue
In honor of John's 30th Birthday
On Friday, the sixth of August
Six o'clock in the evening
The Hunt Residence
125 Springwood Terrace

Please respond by
the twentieth of July

John's 30th

A BLACK-AND-WHITE BARBECUE

for twenty

It seems like every year, we dub a different age "the new thirty." Frankly, I'm all for it. At thirty we finally know a little something about how life works — who we are, what we need, what we want — but the sparks of youth are still flying. Of course, the melding of responsibility and freedom that makes thirty such an exciting time of life also makes designing a good birthday party particularly challenging. Take my client John, for instance. Wishing to declare his independence from fraternity cookouts of the past and also to announce his official entrance into adulthood, he asked me to help him and his wife celebrate his thirtieth with a lively but "proper" dinner, a party that would reinvent his storied entertaining style for more urbane times. The trick would be locating John somewhere on the continuum between a keg party and a wine tasting. But how?

One of my very favorite inspirations for thirtieth-birthday parties are photographs from the honoree's favorite celebrations in years past. There's no better way to get a sense of who someone is and how he or she has both changed and remained the same over time.

At thirty we finally know a little something about how life works, but the sparks of youth are still flying.

It took only a few small piles of snapshots showing John smiling and tending an outdoor grill to help me devise the perfect celebration for his new stage in life: a backyard barbecue fit for black tie. Instead of chuck and chili, lobster and filet mignon would sizzle on the grill; instead of a dusty picnic table adorned with plastic cups, boldly sophisticated lines of black and white would provide a cool backdrop for shimmering crystal drops, twinkling candlelight, deep red roses, and crimson table elements to match; and instead of neon coolers filled with tall boys, sleek kettle grills would brim with roses and ferns and give off tantalizing aromas. In other words, when John's friends received a black, white, and red invitation with a small drawing of a grill announcing a barbecue, they would recognize the work of their old friend John. But when they arrived at this suave, down-home gathering, where the classic color scheme dressed up an extravagantly polished picnic, they would also recognize their new friend John — with decades of youth, wisdom, and change still ahead of him.

Grills 'n' roses

THE ART OF GRILLING is coaxing the purest, strongest, and most essential flavor out of simple ingredients with a little fire. Come to think of it, it's not so different from the art of life itself. So this idea offered the key to dressing up what might otherwise have been a basic birthday cookout and bringing out the best of the unlandscaped field behind John's house. For starters, I used the grill as a motif for the smoking-hot combination of the classic and the casual. A tiny drawing of an open grill enclosed in a black-and-white-checked box at the top of the party invitation gave guests the first hint of this motif. Just as the drawing would expand the way John's friends thought of him, the party would expand the way they thought of that well-loved American institution—the backyard barbecue.

Kettle and hibachi grills (which can be borrowed from friends or purchased inexpensively at a local hardware store) figured into almost every major design element, from furniture to decorations. I filled the standard Weber kettle grills with potting soil to make planters for bountiful Boston ferns, which defined the perimeter of the party space in the yard. In a play

Elegant black-and-white-checked chair covers

MATERIALS

o 1½ to 2 yards fabric per chair (depending on the width of the fabric, this amount could be split to cover two chairs)

o 3 to 4 yards ribbon per chair

o stapler

o hot glue and hot-glue gun

o scissors

METHOD

1. Cut the fabric so that it is two inches wider than the width of the chair and long enough to reach from the seat, up the chair back, and over the top of the chair back down to the floor behind it.

2. With the fabric turned inside out, drape the tailored length of fabric over the chair back, with one end touching the ground behind the chair and the other touching the seat.

3. Staple the fabric (one inch apart) along the lengths of both sides. Remove it from the chair and turn it right side out.

4. Using a glue gun, affix red ribbon to the side and bottom edges of the cover.

5. Place the covers over the chair backs.

on the ordinary cocktail table, I added a stabilizing dirt base to the same black kettle grills and spelled out "30" in rosebuds underneath the grate. I also placed an old steak sauce bottle holding red roses and a few red votives in the center and scattered the repurposed grills about the yard for the perfect drink perches. Perhaps most striking, along with a few red votive candles, I used hibachi grills to make a fabulously fiery centerpiece. Having the small grills lined up at even intervals down the center of the table added to the visual rhythm of the evening's mix. In order to make this centerpiece truly pop, I arranged still more red rosebuds in even lines between the grill grates, so that the bright crimson of the flowers literally rose up in the air like sparks from a flame. Talk about a hot spot! The clean, low lines of the centerpiece accentuated the vision of simple backyard extravagance that inspired the party, and all without interrupting the sight lines of guests talking well into the night across the long tables.

The grill motif of this luminous homestyle party inspired its color scheme as well, and this detail made the centerpiece even more unforgettable. In order to preserve the easy charm of an intimate barbecue in an upscale form, I painted John's trusty old picnic tables in long black and white stripes that evoked the iconic grill marks and bold contrasts every dedicated backyard chef strives for. Placed entirely within the lines of the

MATERIALS

○ 1 hibachi

○ Oasis (floral foam) — enough to fill the bottom of the grill

○ 12 red roses

○ red glass votives with wax inserts

○ charcoal

METHOD

1. Remove the grill grate and fill the hibachi with one-inch-thick soaked Oasis cut to fit the bottom. Cover it with charcoal.

2. Cut the rose stems to about three inches long.

3. Replace the grill grate and arrange the roses in the Oasis along the lines of the grill, with each bloom rising off the grill grate like a flame.

4. Add a single red glass votive in the middle of the grill.

white stripe down the center of the table, the black and red colors of the rose-laden hibachi runner, not to mention the red votives that dotted the spaces between them, made for quite a dramatic palette. To intensify the effect, I extended the black-and-white scheme to the cotton slipcovers I made to spruce up inexpensive black Chiavari chairs (rented ballroom chairs) in a formal take on the basic gingham tablecloth. Like the center-piece and the party as a whole, though, the slipcovers were not complete without a touch of flame red. On the chair covers, this red came in a simple ribbon trimming the edge, but on the table, it took numerous lively forms. Red glass charger plates smoldered beneath the more classic white china, guests hoisted their Red Martinis in tribute to their host, and red glass goblets spiced up a more stately crystal counterpart by its side. Red napkins rolled into a red ribbon ring studded with crimson rose heads added a final zing to each guest's dinner setting, while black, white, and red place cards matching the party invitations beckoned guests to sit down and dig in. The red-rose-and-votive arrangements topping each of the kettle-grill cocktail tables carried the look to all reaches of the yard. Of course, such a concentration of fiery colors and radiant energy always benefits from a cooling, more luxurious touch. To achieve that, I removed the fabric from two old outdoor table umbrellas and draped them in yards of affordable faux-crystal roping and red hanging votives. The result was an intricately crafted outdoor chandelier fit for a king, a great outdoorsman, or both rolled into one: drops of twinkling glass and glowing light hung over the dining table like a suspended meteor shower from a refreshingly design-conscious planet. All in all, it was a perfect setting to celebrate John's long tradition of welcoming friends and family to his trusty grill, but this time with a new fire.

HOW to | ## Enchanting umbrella chandelier

MATERIALS

○ outdoor umbrella with base, used or new

○ several yards of crystal roping, as much as desired (available at lighting supply stores, some craft stores, and online)

○ crystal drops (available at lighting supply stores, some hardware stores, and online)

○ spool wire

○ wire cutters

○ several hanging glass candleholders with votives, as many as desired

○ black spray paint

○ scissors

METHOD

1. Remove the cloth cover from the umbrella with scissors.

2. Using old newspaper or drop cloths to protect your lawn, spray-paint the umbrella frame black.

3. Once it's dry, raise the frame over the designated table and drape with as many strands of crystal roping as you like, going from spoke to spoke around the entire umbrella. Attach them with wire.

4. Accent the roping with crystal drops and hanging candles. Attach them with wire.

NOTE: When candles are used overhead, you might want to consider battery-operated candles for safety purposes.

Rugged but regal

WHEN IT COMES TO THROWING A PARTY for a thirty-year-old man, many people seem to fear delicate textures like soft fabrics and roses. They think of peanut shells underfoot and worn vinyl bar stools and immediately place a call to the local dive bar to reserve a dart board — a tragedy of the first order for those trying to move beyond the good ol' days. In my experience, thirty is the time when men are ready to experiment with new styles and design elements, and adding just a few rugged touches can make even the most delicate textures feel utterly masculine. For John's party, I relied heavily on the velvety feel of rose petals, sleek crystal, and soft cotton slipcovers to create a lush experience of the great outdoors, but I never let the softness of these accents overwhelm. Instead, I incorporated rough-hewn details every step of the way. For instance, rather than spreading fabric over the tables, I let the weathered, painted wood stand on its own as a tribute to the rough-hewn aesthetic at the heart of barbecue culture. Likewise, I substituted the utilitarian steel surfaces of kettle grills for cocktail tables swathed in silk, and the spare, linear grate of a hibachi for crystal vases in the centerpiece. The result was masculine but chic, adventurous but mature, and, perhaps best of all, absolutely no vinyl was used in the making of this party.

HOW to Rose-red napkin rings

MATERIALS

- 3 small rosebuds per napkin ring, with stems trimmed flush
- cardboard paper towel roll
- 2-inch-wide red ribbon
- hot glue and hot-glue gun
- scissors

METHOD

1. Cut the paper towel roll into two-inch sections, making as many rings as needed for the desired number of place settings.

2. Glue the ribbon inside and outside the roll.

3. Dab the ring with hot glue and place a rose on the glue. Let dry.

NOTE: Use silk roses for permanent use.

the TASTE

A grown-up grill

WE SHOULD BE FRANK: men like fire. It is one of the only ingredients that tempts some of them into more refined culinary waters. So it's no surprise that the grill motif that defined the party's look also extended to the bold flavors and deep contrasts at the heart of its four-star menu. It all began with the vivid punch of a Red Martini, whose blazing color heated up conversations as the guests arrived. When the first course was served, "seeing red" took on an entirely different meaning. The dark magenta of sliced beets, with their earthy, vegetal sweetness, paired perfectly with the tangy taste of white goat cheese and crunchy black sesame seeds. For the main course, perfectly grilled steak and lobster from Omaha Steaks and a grilled potato pancake paid unforgettable tribute to the pleasures of putting fine foods on the grate. And last but not least, a few round scoops of Merlot sorbet from Ciao Bella brought a robust spark to the rich black-and-white cookie nestled against it in a martini glass and also to the streaks of white and dark chocolate drizzled against the inside.

When the time came to light the birthday candles on John's birthday cake, which was shaped as a kettle grill and adorned with rose cookies from Eleni's, the evening was already aglow with its own celebratory flame. Was it just me, or did the crowd hesitate a minute before blowing it out?

the Menu

BEET-AND-GOAT-CHEESE SALAD WITH TOASTED BLACK SESAME SEEDS WITH RASPBERRY AND VODKA REDUCTION

GRILLED LOBSTER TAIL AND FILET MIGNON ON A BED OF SAUTÉED WILD MUSHROOMS WITH A YUKON GOLD POTATO PANCAKE

MERLOT SORBET WITH A BLACK-AND-WHITE COOKIE IN A DARK-AND WHITE-CHOCOLATE WEB

GRILL CAKE WITH ROSE COOKIES

Blazing red martini

2 ounces fresh blood orange juice (strained)
2 ounces Belvedere Pomarancza Vodka
splash of Grand Marnier
1½ ounces Grenadine
red-colored sugar

POUR all the ingredients except the sugar into a
cocktail shaker with ice.

SHAKE and strain into a martini glass rimmed with
red sugar.

White chocolate-garnished martini glass

THIS CAN BE DONE ONE DAY IN ADVANCE

white chocolate chips
double boiler
pastry bag — or a sturdy Ziploc bag with one (very!)
small corner snipped off after it has been filled
martini glasses

FILL the bottom level of the double boiler with
water and melt the chips in the top.

POUR the melted chips into a pastry bag.

SQUEEZE the chocolate onto the inside of each
glass in a thin stream, swirling the glass to create
any design you please. Let it set.

NOTE: To help the chocolate set, place the glass in
the refrigerator.

the SCENT

A savory sizzle

THE AROMA OF A GOOD GRILL FIRE can have startling effects. I've seen more than my share of curious bypassers peer over a backyard fence after catching a sweet, smoky whiff of charcoal and seared beef. It lures forth memories of childhood summers as surely as it lures hungry guests to the table. At the risk of drawing uninvited guests, John's birthday barbecue came complete with its own intoxicating fragrance. As lobster and filet mignon sizzled over the flame, the air was filled with the buzzing anticipation of the delectable meal to come and memories of John's much-touted cookouts from years past. Whenever I use deeply familiar scents at birthday parties, I like to add newer scents, too, that will change the way guests respond to them in the future, in effect marking them with an association with that one day. That's why I made sure the red roses that heated up the look of the party were abundant enough to perfume the air as well. This sweet, subtle addition might not have overwhelmed the aroma of burning embers and grilled lobster, but I guarantee it lingers on in the guests' memories of John's unforgettable celebration.

Peaceful, easy feeling

IF TURNING THIRTY promises the best of both worlds, I can't imagine a more fitting sound track for John's backyard shindig on this pivotal birthday than a little bit of country and a little bit of rock 'n' roll. Favorite hits from his college days, such as the Allman Brothers' "Melissa" and the Eagles' "Peaceful, Easy Feeling," bolstered the laid-back, familiar vibe crucial to any backyard party, while songs from more recent rotation, like Big and Rich's "Big Time" and Aerosmith's cover of the classic "Baby, Please Don't Go," brought a more upbeat edge to the mix.

One of the most important things music can do for a party is create a distinctly different rhythm for different parts of the evening. In this respect it's not so unlike working a good grill: you know where your hot spot is and where your cool spot is, and you know when to use each one. Part of growing up is knowing when to let other people take over, so John happily entrusted a hired DJ with a song list of must-plays, and instead of running around all night looking for a stack of homemade CDs, he left it to a professional and enjoyed the time with his friends.

Medium-tempo songs, such as Counting Crows' "Goodnight L.A.," the Wallflowers' "One Headlight," and the Traveling Wilburys' "Last Night," heated up the conversations as guests arrived. Over dinner, slower songs, like Eric Clapton's unplugged version of "Layla," Lyle Lovett's "Pontiac," and Tom Petty's "Into the Great Wide Open," smoldered in the air. Right after John blew out his candles, the music struck up with the song he describes as his "anthem," Joe Walsh's "Life's Been Good" — a great birthday send-off for any age. Finally, with nothing to do but dance the night away under the bright stars, things got cooking again with Van Morrison's "Wild Night," Kid Rock's "Cowboy," and Gretchen Wilson's "Here for the Party." At the end of the night, as John said good-bye to all his friends, and John Prine's "Angel from Montgomery" cooled the energy level once again, it was plain to see that life would be good to John for a long time yet.

- Don't panic if you run out of time before the meat defrosts. To defrost your frozen lobster or sealed meat quickly, place it in a sink filled with cold water — within half an hour, it will be ready for the grill.

- After grilling meat, remove it from the grill and let it sit for three to five minutes. This helps lock in all the juices. Keep in mind that meat still cooks once removed from the grill, so pull your meat off the grill a few moments before it's fully cooked (or reaches the desired preparedness).

- Don't throw away an old, rusty grill. They make fun and original planters for a deck or patio and last forever. Be sure to add gravel to the bottom of your grill planter for proper drainage.

- To add a great smoky wood flavor to your charcoal grill, soak mesquite wood chips in water for a half hour and sprinkle them in among the hot coals. Mesquite chips are usually available where you buy charcoal.

- If the weather isn't perfect for outdoor grilling, add a little Liquid Smoke to your marinade and grill indoors instead. Liquid Smoke adds a touch of outdoor grilling flavor, even if you have to cook in your oven. Also, indoor grilling is possible year-round, not just in the summer months. To get those signature outdoor-grill marks, try using an iron grill on your stove top. In addition to meat, try corn, pineapple, and asparagus.

- Think outside the box when dreaming up a birthday cake: cupcakes, cookies, or even doughnuts are a fun alternative to a traditional cake. A smaller dessert used in abundance makes for a fabulous presentation. Have fun and stack the cupcakes or doughnuts on tiered cake trays for a unique birthday presentation.

- Remember that the dessert is the last course (and the last moment for some parties), so create a dessert that really captures the essence of your party — both in color and in style. For a black-white-and-red-themed party, try Merlot sorbet in a chocolate-garnished martini glass with a black-and-white cookie. This truly combines the casual with the elegant and leaves a lasting impression. Remember, it's all in the presentation.

- Serve two different types of desserts, giving one to some guests and the other to other guests. It will create additional conversation, and guests will be urged to share.

- Create a colorful backyard "dining room" by painting stripes on an ordinary picnic table (the natural lines of the table make it easy to paint) to match the "stripes" of the grill. Several colorful stripes look great for a kid's party.

- When entertaining outdoors, don't forget about your uninvited guests . . . the bugs. Spray the area the day before to help ward off pests. Local companies provide party sprays that really do the trick. Organic, nontoxic sprays are available. Save A Tree has a spray called a Mosquito/Surface Insect Application that is derived from garlic. It is effective for two to four days.

CONCLUSION

Memories in the making

SOMETIME TOWARD THE END OF DINNER, as John and his guests savored the last sweet forkfuls of lobster and steak, dusk settled over the yard. The heat of the bright September day cooled to darkness, with only the glow of candles dangling from above and dotting the tabletop to light the scene. It might have been an illusion — one of those special effects of happy circumstances that transform the mood of a good party — but in that flickering light, John swore the entire party seemed different, and I had to agree that it was not just the Red Martinis. The buzz of laughter and conversation rose in pitch, the red of the roses and ribbons looked deeper, the black-and-white stripes and checks appeared more striking, and every dot of firelight danced more vividly in the crystal's reflection. Just as John had transformed himself before the very eyes of his oldest friends, the party, too, seemed to have transformed itself in his honor. As he blew out the candles on his thirtieth-birthday cake, it was easy to envision the many good, long years that lay ahead.

Alleyne's 40th

TURNING OVER A NEW LEAF
WITH OLD FRIENDS

for sixteen

It was not so long ago that turning forty was thought of as something to dread rather than something to celebrate. Announcing the accomplishment of this milestone in life was as good as proclaiming for all to hear the growth of a spare tire around the waist or an early gray hair. My, how times have changed. As we all live longer and healthier lives, forty is not only an age to celebrate, it is often the very first moment when we know who we are and how to honor the things we value most deeply in life. For some this might mean kicking off a fresh start with a spirited tribute to change, and for others it might mean reflecting on the most enduring sources of happiness throughout the years. One of my favorite things about a good fortieth-birthday party is that it usually strikes a particular balance between the two, making for an almost quintessential celebration of all the surprises and the continuities that blend together to make every life unique.

Perhaps the first time I really recognized this quality was when I was planning a party for a client named Alleyne. Recently divorced, she told me that she wanted to celebrate the excitement of turning over a new leaf with all the friends who had supported her in the process. I knew that every element of the event had to exude the optimism for growth and change I saw in Alleyne's eyes, and I started thinking of wildflowers and bold colors (and a recent episode of *Desperate Housewives*). But when I learned that she'd met almost all of her lifelong friends as a young girl taking sewing lessons one summer at her parents' country club, it hit me: every new leaf grows from deep roots. The decor for this party would have to capture the retro and the modern, the novel and the traditional, the new bloom and its steadfast stem all at once. Like a great dress pattern, the old-fashioned infuses contemporary innovation. And so, this ode to growth and life began with the stately grounds of her family's club. I saw its grand old dining room decked in the bright, cheerful colors and quirky geometric patterns that give a vintage picqué sundress its modern verve. I saw yards and yards of girlish grosgrain and satin ribbons tailored to trim every detail with a neat accent, wrapping up life as a gift. And most important, I saw dozens of freshly cut calla lilies and hydrangeas — Alleyne's favorite flowers — bringing the same sense of vitality, growth, and poise that made her so radiant in the lovely glow of the future. Life would, without a doubt, continue to regale her and her friends in such elegant fashion, however they evolved in time.

As we all live longer and healthier lives, forty is not only an age to celebrate, it is often the very first moment when we know who we are and how to honor the things we value most deeply in life.

Perky as a pair of pumps and a matching purse

ONE IMAGE SENT ME OVER THE EDGE: Alleyne as a teenager in the 1980s, lounging by the country club pool in her teenybopper (as she described, "Belinda Carlisle") bathing suit while hand-stitching the letter *A* onto a new batch of retro 1950s-style twinsets for her big back-to-school fashion debut. (She gives suburban girlie culture a good name.) Inspired by her snapshots and memories, I set about to open up a special time capsule for her big fortieth birthday. I made sure that every element had the retro zip and modern flair Alleyne was famous for. First I started with some preppy Lilly Pulitzer colors (bright pink and chartreuse green) to complement the sunny golf-and-poolside vibe of the club. To draw out a more formal and retro element, I added trimmings in basic black. The whole room bounced with springtime enthusiasm like a very meticulously arranged Easter basket.

First I set some simple square tables with formal black cloths and festive pink fringe. Bright pink chairs were adorned with kelly green cushions, while frosted-pink votive holders were trimmed with crystal-studded fabric and placed next to tall green candles. I added a simple and pretty bouquet of jade roses to each table to complete the tailored look. Over at the

main dining table, I continued with a refined and feminine floral theme, only now the blooms were shaped into pom-poms and swags and attached to chair backs. Tall lilies and leaning tulips were designed in an architectural and European style, so that they seemed to be reaching out from their vases. In among all the little bouquets and charming explosions of flora were roses, hyacinths, hydrangeas, tulips, peonies, orchids, and lilies. The table was set with a pale pink satin cloth and trimmed with green and black-and-white polka-dot ribbons. These same ribbons were used to accent candleholders, vases, little gift boxes, and napkins, and a few of the pastel ribbons also draped over the chair backs.

Since Alleyne met half of her girlfriends in sewing class, I couldn't resist a little needle-and-thread charm. I topped spools of pink thread with little clusters of jewels, and pinned a threaded needle through a handwritten pink name card. The effect was very tailored, to say the least. Place settings (by Marc Blackwell) revolved around mod polka-dot martini glasses and swirling striped champagne and water glasses. Green napkins were pressed, folded, and accented with ribbons and a brooch (for the ladies) and cuff links (for the gents). When Alleyne walked in wearing a bright pink eyelet dress and a newly bronzed country club tan, she quite literally pulled the whole room together: a glowing centerpiece of the marvelous and mannered decor.

Dressing up basic glass votives and vases with fun little accessories is an economical way to add style and personality to any table. You can find both the votives and the accessories at most fabric stores or floral supply warehouses, so with little fuss and lots of options you can add a unique, magical light to your event. Once you've got your votives, pick out some fun accessories for them, like sparkly trim, ribbon, buttons, crystals, or even seashells. Affix them to the outside of the votive candleholders with a high-temperature hot glue or craft glue. Add a tea light candle to each of the votives and you're ready to go.

I absolutely love using calla lilies for any party in need of flowers with an elegant, modern look. In order to simplify the process, I've included the basic steps to making four wonderful arrangements that will never fail to dazzle, each one designated by the type of vase it requires.

LARGE GLOBE VASE

Globe vases create a perfect opportunity to bend and twist calla lilies to desired shapes, which creates a breathtaking optical illusion when the vase is viewed from different angles. Whatever the size of your bowl, fill it with water up to one-quarter its volume. Place the calla lilies inside the vase one at a time, shaping each one to follow the curvature of the vase by gently squeezing and bending it along the stem with your fingers, which moves the water inside it to mold it into place. Let the flowers extend one-quarter of the way up inside the vase for a chic, architectural feeling.

LARGE SLIM RECTANGLE VASE

A variation on the large globe vase arrangement, this one maintains the clean lines while adding in a few extra flowers for a more light-hearted accent. Begin by filling the vase three-quarters full with water. Carefully mold the stems of the lilies into place with your fingers to any desired shape, but keep the look tailored for the best effect. Calla lilies hold a great deal of water, so even if the base of the flower comes out of the water, it will remain hydrated. For a more natural look, add carnations, orchids, or anthuriums, which also keep well without water. But make sure to use an odd number of flowers to create a loose sense of flow!

MEDIUM SLIM CYLINDER VASE

This multidimensional arrangement offers an energetic changeup for the eye. Begin by filling the vase three-quarters full with water. As with the large slim rectangle vase, gently mold the lilies with your fingers until you achieve the desired shape. Then add hydrangea or viburnum floret heads at water level for a stunning two-tiered effect.

SMALL RECTANGLE VASE

This arrangement uses smaller lilies to fit the scale of the vase, and it works well especially on cocktail tables or in tighter party spaces. Begin by gathering three miniature calla lilies. Bunch them together so that their blooms are at staggered levels and secure them with floral tape. Cover the tape with a small leaf and fasten it with a pearl-head pin. I often match the pinhead color to the colors of the party space for a fun touch. Cut the stems evenly, place them at an angle in the vase, and voilà!

Floating on a cloud of floral-scented bliss

JUST SHY OF DUMPING a wheelbarrow's worth of the season's first lawn trimmings next to the dining tables, I did my very best to pack Alleyne's dinner full of that inimitable and delightfully fresh aroma of springtime at the club. I filled the country club dining room with bunches and bunches of feminine and fragrant spring flowers and then simply let the blooms do the talking. Bouquets of baby hydrangeas exuded the energizing fragrance of newborn blossoms. The sweet scent of tulips made a perfect match for the trays of Blushing Ladies whizzing by in waiters' hands, while the fresh scent of their stems mingled nicely with the Cucumber Lime Saketinis. And for a dainty but retro touch, I couldn't resist the lure of the calla lily. I also filled glass vases with peonies and watched them fall into place in their own romantic and fluttery fashion. Button mums, carnations, and roses were arranged in spherical bunches and ladylike swags and attached to the backs of the dining chairs. Finally, bunches of pink hyacinths chimed into this virtual orchestra of aromatic flowers with their signature springtime perfume. Though hyacinths can boast quite a heady fragrance in tight quarters, when you're entertaining in a large and airy room, these elegant air fresheners make a magnificent and subtle statement. There was no doubt that Alleyne and her guests would float away on a leisurely cloud of floral-scented bliss.

Floral chair backs

MATERIALS

○ Oasis floral foam and IGLU holder (a sturdy plastic cage filled with floral foam; it comes in various sizes)

○ flowers (green button mums, soft-yellow carnations, jade roses)

○ Galex leaves

○ low-temp hot glue and hot-glue gun

○ wire

○ wide ribbon

METHOD

1. Soak the Oasis in water until it is completely saturated.

2. Cut each flower, leaving a two-inch stem.

3. Starting in the center of the IGLU cage, push the flowers fully into the Oasis one at a time, making sure to completely cover the Oasis with a solid half sphere of flowers.

4. Using your hot-glue gun, attach the Galex leaves to the flat side of the cage to completely mask the plastic. It's best to overlap the leaves.

5. Attach the floral arrangements to the backs of the chairs with wire, leaving a little space between each.

6. Wrap a wide ribbon around the top of each half sphere and allow it to flow to the ground.

NOTE: To create the swag floral chair back, use Oasis garland cages (which interlock) instead of the spherical holders.

Soft as a petal

MOST PEOPLE CHOOSE FLOWERS based on their unique look, color, or fragrance. Too often we forget that one of the most crucial characteristics of a blossom is its texture. A whole mood can be established by the feel of the foliage. I've created wild, futuristic looks with the help of an abundance of exotic, unusual flora, and more minimal decor with boxes of glossy grasses and matte velvet reeds. Alleyne's tailored but feminine birthday called for lots of fluttering floral petals all nicely arranged in smooth glass vases. I started with perhaps the most feminine of all flowers, the ever-so-delicate peony. Peonies seem to bounce gently in the breeze like fairy wings. In keeping with the feminine vibe, I added fluffy carnations and hydrangeas to the tables and chair backs. To contrast with these delicate and ruffled bouquets, I mixed in bunches of glossy tulips, velvety orchids, and smooth calla lilies. I even popped in a few bouquets of funky, tubular hyacinth for good measure. This mix of fluttery and smooth surfaces could also be found in the table dressings. Tailored tablecloths gave way to fringed edges, and satin ribbons dangled from bushy bouquets. Sleek vases held chunky green stems, and shimmering jewels accentuated neat, pressed napkins. The final effect was a truly feminine one that projected both the flowing and the finished at the same time.

Piano Dan to the rescue

WHEN I THINK OF "COUNTRY CLUB MUSIC," a scene right out of a hip sixties movie comes to mind. I see a tuxedo-clad piano man tickling the ivories over in the corner, a martini permanently poised on top of his white baby grand. We no longer live in a world where regular people spend a sunny afternoon drinking martinis in a piano bar, but there's always a way to reach into the past and pull from it just those elements that we need for the present. For Alleyne's country club birthday party, I found a genuine bona fide piano man to entertain the dining ladies and gents. This particular old-school entertainer, named simply Piano Dan, had traded in his white tux for a spiffy ivory linen suit. Piano Dan played the coolest, prettiest background music while sipping on decidedly alcohol-free lemonades. He was a real crooner, too — Harry Connick Jr., eat your heart out.

Some settings and occasions really benefit from the personality of a little live music, and Piano Dan created just the right atmosphere at this swank soirée. A good piano player can lift the spirits in any room while maintaining a formal, and in this case feminine, vibe. Many of them build their businesses largely by word of mouth, so finding one is as simple as asking trusted friends or a local bar with music you like for a recommendation. In fact, the country club management was so excited by the positive response to the music at Alleyne's party that they decided to dust that baby grand off and grab one of Piano Dan's business cards.

Rustic simplicity

OKAY, I ADMIT IT. Colston Bassett Stilton, Finnan Haddock, and Bourride Antiboise sound more like names from a New England prep school than a description of dinner. But what these English, Scottish, and French culinary delicacies have in common is a deep association with a particular place and a rustic simplicity that makes them ripe for reinvention. Along with the refined flavors they boast, this combination of custom and innovation set just the right tone for Alleyne's tradition-tweaking fortieth-birthday menu. After sipping on cool Cucumber Lime Saketinis, a sweet Blushing Lady, or a rich Liquid Chocolate Martini — each of which brought out the party's nouveau vintage color scheme rather deliciously — guests embarked on an intrepid tour of reimagined provincial cuisine they would not soon forget.

The meal began with the Finnan Haddock, a Scottish specialty from the hamlet of Findon that entails splitting, brining, and smoking the fish for a robust, billowing flavor. But this was no ordinary Finnan Haddock: it was served over a smooth, creamy potato-and-leek soup and topped with a spray of crispy-fried matchstick leeks for a more modern study in contrasts. The salad that followed was no less chic in its spare interpretation of a classic English cheese from the renowned Colston Bassett dairy in Nottinghamshire. With just a dusting of this famous fresh and mild white stilton, the tender baby Bibb lettuce, smoky toasted walnuts, and sweet garlic croutons offered an unexpected sense of play among all the different tastes. But nothing could compare to the Bourride Antiboise that arrived for the entrée. Bourride is a classic fish stew native to the Provençal city of Antibes, which stands as a landmark of coastal country cooking. For Alleyne's party we served it with a few contemporary enhancements, from a mélange of roasted potatoes and soft baby leeks redolent with saffron to a smattering of plump mussels fresh from the Canadian Atlantic. It was a far-reaching menu that fit right into the familiar walls of the family club; it was a blending of the Old World and the New; it was adventurous but grounded; it represented the best of everything to come.

the Menu

LEEK-AND-POTATO SOUP,
FINNAN HADDOCK, AND
CRISPY LEEK STICKS

BABY BIBB LETTUCE, COLSTON
BASSETT STILTON, TOASTED
WALNUTS, AND SWEET GARLIC
CROUTONS

BOURRIDE ANTIBOISE WITH
PEEWEE MONKFISH, PRINCE
EDWARD ISLAND MUSSELS,
ROASTED SAFFRON POTATOES,
AND BABY LEEKS

SQUARE GIFT-BOX CAKE

Then again, the four-tiered birthday cake (by Confetti Cakes) that capped off the evening was pretty spectacular, too. Perched like a stack of gifts yet to be opened, its pink, green, and dark chocolate icing made for a neat play on the party's decor. And even better, the unforgettably light vanilla cake inside only confirmed that some of life's sweetest gifts are the most unexpected.

Cucumber lime saketini

2 ounces cold sake
1 ounce cucumber juice
½ ounce fresh lime juice
splash of simple syrup
lime slice, for garnish

POUR all of the ingredients except the lime into a cocktail shaker with ice. Shake and strain into a martini glass.

GARNISH with a slice of lime.

Blushing lady

2 ounces vodka
1 ounce pink grapefruit juice
1 ounce PAMA pomegranate liqueur
lemon wedge
coarse sugar, for garnish

RUB a wedge of lemon around the rim of a martini glass and dip the glass into a plate of coarse sugar. Set it aside. Pour the remaining ingredients into a cocktail shaker with ice. Shake and strain into the garnished martini glass.

Liquid chocolate martini

2 ounces vodka
1 ounce dark chocolate liqueur
splash of hazelnut liqueur
lemon wedge
crushed M&M's, for garnish

RUB a wedge of lemon around the rim of a martini glass and dip the glass into a plate of crushed M&M's. Set it aside. Pour the remaining ingredients into a cocktail shaker with ice. Shake and strain into the garnished martini glass.

- To test the freshness of a rose before you buy it, lightly squeeze the bud. If it's firm, it's fresh; if it's soft, don't buy it.

- Whether the party is formal or casual, always make sure to state the dress attire on the invite. It takes the guesswork out for your guests and also creates uniformity to complete the look of the party.

- To make a rose look fuller for an arrangement, gently blow into the head of the rose to separate the petals.

- I like to seat couples at parties separately — it encourages conversation at dinner. Then at dessert I ask all the gentlemen to change seats again, allowing for more mixing and mingling.

- When entertaining at a long common table, the host or hostess should be seated in the center with his or her back to the wall.

- If hydrangea petals are starting to wilt, submerge the entire flower in cool water for ten minutes to rehydrate it. Hydrangeas "drink" through their petals as well as their stems.

- Music should escalate throughout the evening, with its style changing every fifteen to twenty minutes. This will help maintain the flow of the party.

- To open a closed lily, place it in a bucket of warm water, cover it with a plastic bag, and place it in indirect sunlight. This works like a hot house and opens the blooms quickly.

- When roses are purchased in bulk, the guard petals, or outer petals, often get bruised or broken. Simply pinch the damaged ones off and the rose will look fresh and last longer.

- Don't let flowers go to waste. Have your caterer arrange for the wait staff to remove the flowers and wrap them in tissue with a bow for guests to take home.

You must remember this...

IN REMEMBRANCE OF ALLEYNE'S BIRTHDAY celebration, each guest took home a tiny box of Fauchon chocolates and one sparkling accessory — brooches for the women and cuff links and tie tacks for the men. A keepsake might seem like a simple enough thing, but what is remarkable about these small gifts is the way they meant different things to different guests. One of Alleyne's best girlfriends devoured the chocolates on the spot, kissed her friend good-bye, and shouted, "Life is sweet!" Another girlfriend took one look at the gold lettering on the chocolates' pink box and decided spontaneously to join Alleyne on a trip to Paris, home of the revered Fauchon shop. The brooches garnered just as much interest. One friend recalled a dress she and Alleyne had made together as girls and thought how perfect the brooch would look with it, while another friend mailed hers back to Alleyne a month later along with a beautiful new evening coat she'd sewn for her for future nights of glamour and romance. Each gift carried with it the reassurances of the past combined with the possibilities of the future — just like Alleyne herself.

Cynthia's 50th

A WHITE-ON-WHITE DINNER PARTY

for thirty-five

If there is ever a time to insist that living well is the best revenge, it's at a fiftieth-birthday party. That's right about the time we might thank our stars that life isn't all that short after all but realize it was best to avoid the cheap wine anyway. So when a client of mine named Cynthia asked if I would help her design a grand fiftieth-birthday party at her waterfront summer home using only the color white, I loved the idea. What could be more fitting? This simple color theme combines the classic fanfare of a starched tuxedo shirt with the relaxed chic of a simple strand of pearls. In a word, it is timeless. Like a fresh canvas, white tables, drapes, chairs, and accents would make the perfect backdrop for Cynthia, her husband, and her group of thirty-five friends and family members to both conjure up their favorite times past and imagine all the fabulous new things to come. That experience, after all, is the essence of a well-spent birthday.

I got my greatest inspiration from the grounds that I would later deck in white chiffon, gardenias, and buoyant pearly baubles. The property behind Cynthia's house, set on a small island, looked out over the lake surrounding it and also at a series of romantic stone ponds scattered around the perimeter of a covered arcade. It was screaming out for a seriously

If there is ever a time to insist that living well is the best revenge, it's at a fiftieth-birthday party.

dramatic unveiling, which I imagined right then and there: guests would receive faux pearl–trimmed invitations on iridescent white paper announcing the all-white dress code with a hint of mystery. When the day of the party finally came, I would arrange a small boat to transport them, as if magically, to the extravagant scene of Cynthia's party. Once on Cynthia's epic garden terrace, they would indulge in champagne and hors d'oeuvres while mingling amid grand stone columns and flowing chiffon curtains. In the spell of Jazz Age glamour that came over me, I couldn't remember if *The Great Gatsby* ended happily or not. Oh, well — this celebratory reinvention of its elegance most certainly would.

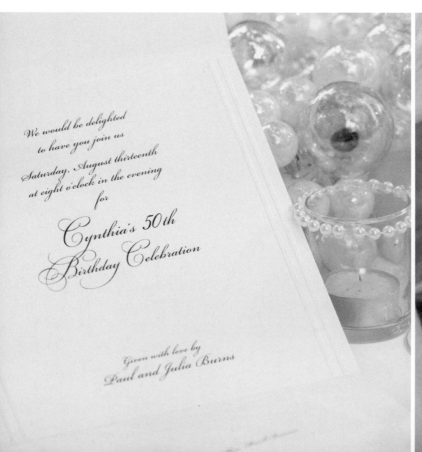

We would be delighted
to have you join us
Saturday, August thirteenth
at eight o'clock in the evening
for
Cynthia's 50th
Birthday Celebration

Given with love by
Paul and Julia Burns

Baubles and bubbles

AS I DREW UP THE PLANS for the exuberant *Gatsby* glam I had in mind, tiny golden champagne bubbles kept coming to mind. To amplify this vision, I used spherical shapes in abundance: faux pearls, holiday baubles, polka-dot patterns on frosted glass hurricane lamps, and big, delicious fondant balls that seemed to simply roll off the white (of course!) tiered birthday cake. But the beauty of this theme is more than just how beautiful it looks. Strands of faux pearls are inexpensive, can be purchased by the yard or loose, and really lend a bathtub-gin kind of swing without disrupting a formal party atmosphere. I used them everywhere: attached to the border of the satin tablecloth, draped in loops over the chiffon-covered chairs, tied in strands around each napkin, and glued to the edges of each invitation, place card, votive candleholder, and candelabra lampshade. To continue this bouncy theme in the centerpiece, I decorated simple white candelabras with clear, white, and opal Christmas ornaments, and accented the lampshades with dangling pearls. Waterford

Wedgwood china, flatware, and crystal glasses added a cool, classic touch. Elegant gardenias and white rose heads brought an even softer focus to this cool, peaceful look. I created custom polka-dot hurricane lamps for extra candles, with an end result that was classic but overflowing with bubbly charm. A formal party of this kind needed a little bounce in its step, and the ecstatic upward rush of those bubbles in the glass paid the perfect tribute to Cynthia's own effervescence.

Pearl-ornament table runner

MATERIALS

- white Styrofoam sheets, 6 to 8 inches wide and as long as your dining table.

- Christmas ornaments with wire stems in assorted sizes (½ inch, 1 inch, etc.). I used white, pearl, opal, and clear ornaments. This runner calls for approximately 25 to 30 ornaments for each foot of Styrofoam.

- fresh gardenias and white roses (optional: some hurricane lamps or candelabras)

METHOD

1. Cut the Styrofoam in the shape of a runner to fit your table. It does not need to be cut straight; I created a fun wavy effect.

2. Arrange your ornaments on the Styrofoam in a decorative pattern, paying attention to mixing up the sizes and colors throughout.

3. Snip the stems two to three inches long and push the wire into the Styrofoam. Keep the ornaments side by side, touching one another until the runner is completely covered except for a few open spots for hurricane lamps or candelabras. (If you can't find ornaments with wires, you can use wireless ornaments and glue them in place.)

4. Accent the runner with gardenias and white rose heads.

A pearly tablecloth border

MATERIALS

- wide (at least 3-inch), durable ribbon *without* wire edges (wire-edged ribbon is very hard to lay flat) in white or ivory. (You don't want a sheer or delicate ribbon for this project — thick and sturdy is the way to go here.)

- strands of imitation white and ivory pearls in a variety of sizes. These are available at your local craft or fabric store — and during or after Christmas, when stores practically give them away.

- hot glue and hot-glue gun

- pins

METHOD

1. Measure out enough ribbon to go around the entire perimeter of the table.

2. Beginning at one edge of the ribbon, glue strands of pearls along the entire length of the ribbon. Glue more strands right next to these and continue until the entire ribbon is covered in various-size pearls.

3. Pin the finished pearl ribbon to the edge of the tablecloth along the entire perimeter.

Frosted polka-dot hurricane lamps

MATERIALS

- glass hurricane lamps (glass cylinder vases can be substituted)
- round stickers, approximately one inch in diameter (from any office supply store)
- glass-frosting spray or etching acid (available in the spray-paint section of your hardware store)
- strands of faux pearls
- white pillar candles
- hot glue and hot-glue gun
- rubbing alcohol

METHOD

1. Clean the glass thoroughly with rubbing alcohol.
2. Place stickers on the glass in a random pattern.
3. Spray the whole hurricane lamp evenly with glass-frosting spray.
4. Once the lamp is dry, remove the stickers to reveal clear round "windows."
5. Glue a strand of faux pearls around the top edge of the glass hurricane lamp.
6. Place a white pillar candle in the center of each lamp.

Sheer elegance

WHENEVER I AM DECORATING WITH PEARLS, I find I never want to put them down. I love reaching elbow deep into a big box filled with pearls. There is something so smooth and cool about the surface of a pearl that is like nothing else. For Cynthia's party, I wanted guests to feel that pearly softness all around them. In addition to having pearls spilling over the edges of every surface, I used swatches and swatches of beautiful pearly-white chiffon to create billowing curtains and feminine chair covers. The chiffon gave the party an airy, sensual feel. The curtains also helped create an intimate dining area while framing the distant landscape with soft white curves of fabric and never blocking the view. I used bands of ornaments to hold the drapes in place and a final pearly touch: a satin tablecloth trimmed with a wide faux pearl–covered ribbon. This simple upgrade from a fancy white tablecloth added a glossy, sexy feeling to the whole setting.

Champagne-infused

THERE IS NOTHING I LOVE MORE than the elegance of a pristine white china plate, but cover it in all-white foods and you have a recipe for blandness. Whenever I plan a party with a major stylistic theme, I try to interpret the essence of that theme in a few different ways to express it to the best possible effect. This means no white noise and no white dinners. When I planned the menu for Cynthia's party, I tried to use flavors that were as simple and refined as the classic white decor with accents of white that stood out among a subtle palette of colors. To give it all a bounce, I incorporated the buoyant sparkle of champagne, which rounded out the party's luxe white look, into every bite on the three-course menu. And for that culinary *Tutera touch,* I served each dish with a flute of the perfect champagne to match.

Guests began with a salad of white endive, bright mâche, and crunchy sliced radishes in a champagne vinaigrette. The faint spiciness and delicate texture of each elemental ingredient tickled the taste buds with festive intrigue. Another delicately textured dish, seafood crêpes with lobster-champagne sauce, followed with a soft and extravagant sweetness and just a hint of pale color. Then the calming scent of vanilla and champagne announced an offering of poached pears, whose mellow sweetness and light ingredients left plenty of room for the grand finale. No threat of blandness here! An exquisite three-tiered white fondant cake from Carlo's Bakery brought the entire meal together in an irresistible tribute to the guest of honor. Served with dessert champagne aflutter with bubbles, and covered in fondant balls echoing the pearls and baubles of this striking affair, it inspired us all to savor the sweet rewards of life.

the Menu

ENDIVE, MÂCHE, AND RADISH SALAD WITH CHAMPAGNE VINAIGRETTE

VEUVE CLICQUOT 1998 GOLD LABEL BRUT

SEAFOOD CRÊPES WITH LOBSTER-CHAMPAGNE SAUCE

LAURENT-PERRIER 1990 GRAND SIÈCLE

POACHED PEARS WITH VANILLA AND CHAMPAGNE

DOM PERIGNON 1995 ROSE

PEARL WHITE–BAUBLE CAKE

the SOUND

Dramatic entrances . . . and exits

A DRAMATIC AND REMOTE SETTING such as this one has enough inherent glamour to wow guests, even in complete silence. But why not add a little music to accompany the oohs and aahs? So, as the guests rounded the bend to Cynthia's stunning terrace, they could hear the ever-so-subtle strains of a harp playing in the distance. Once the dramatic entrance had made its impact, we switched musical gears for the first round of champagne with a little Cole Porter and other up-tempo Jazz Age classics. The harpist returned to her strumming as the dining commenced. After the toasts had been made (with no music playing, of course), a jazz quartet kicked in with flapper favorites, sending this *Gatsby* fantasy to new heights of kicking and shimmying madness. (When you are planning to have live music in an outdoor setting, be sure to hold a rehearsal beforehand to establish the best location for achieving optimal acoustics.) As the evening wound down past midnight, guests wandered across the lawn to the sounds of a more genteel (less roaring) 1920s jazzy repertoire.

the SCENT

Glamorous gardenias and romantic roses

THERE ARE A NUMBER OF BENEFITS to working with a design premise as simple as the color white. One of my favorites is the way it allows me to indulge guests' senses in nonvisual ways without overwhelming them. Since I love to decorate birthday parties with the honorees' favorite flowers, I already had a plan for Cynthia's special day. The perfume of roses and gardenias filled the air, adding a sensual accent to the white background. Gardenias — the same flower that accessorized those amazing dresses women wore to glamorous parties in the twenties — dotted the table runner from end to end; and white rose heads popped up here and there in aromatic unison. The final floral detail was a single gardenia accenting each napkin set.

TUTERA tips

○ For a more whimsical and romantic candlelight design, make sure you have candles in a variety of sizes and shapes — from low votives to pillar candles to tall tapered candles on candelabras — and be sure to have extras on hand in case they burn down too quickly. You can also rent mechanical candles that are battery-operated.

○ When pairing wine or champagne with each course, provide guests with individual menus naming the particular champagne they're enjoying with each dish.

○ Champagne is not just for drinking! Add it to light sauces and fish dishes in place of wine for an irresistible twist on an ordinary meal.

○ Use place cards for all dinner parties, small or large. This lets the guests know that you took the time to think about the seating and socializing. It also creates a more comfortable environment so guests don't have to wander around looking for a seat or wondering where they should sit.

○ Music for a dinner party should never be overpowering. Opt for light, soft background music to set the tone for the evening, and play it from the moment the first guest arrives to the moment the last guest departs.

○ Picking one great color and using it in abundance makes a strong visual statement. Buying in bulk makes the contents of your wallet more abundant, too!

○ White is no longer just for weddings. When any celebration calls for a clean design and a crisp, sophisticated atmosphere, even Diddy knows it can't be beat.

○ Always remember that what your guests wear will contribute to the feel of your party, so don't be shy when deciding on a dress code. Extending the color white to the dress code for an all-white party may seem like a lot to ask of guests, but more often than not a dress code of any kind makes guests feel like part of the excitement of their environment, and it always starts up conversations.

○ Remember how drab that big old gym looked at your high school dance? It wasn't just the bleachers and retired jerseys that gave it that look. It was also the size of the room. A party in tight quarters always looks better than a party scattered across too much space, so if you're out in the open, define the perimeter of your setting with decorations.

○ When staffing your party, make sure to request one waiter per ten guests. For a more formal affair, figure one and a half to two waiters per ten guests.

Fifty good reasons for a party

PERHAPS THE MOST EXCITING ASPECT of Cynthia's party was the amazing weather. Mother Nature usually helps me out in a pinch, but this time she went overboard. We had been dreading a flat-out rainfall, but just before the guests arrived, a romantic mist rolled in, engulfing the base of the stone columns and floating like wispy clouds over the dark ponds. It was as if we'd paid a special-effects crew to install a fog machine! The picture was complete. But even as I enjoyed this good fortune and hoped it foretold wonderful things for Cynthia, it also made me realize how important it is to create something special with whatever materials we have, whether it's a lovely drift of mist, a lakeside view, or just a few strands of pearls and a bolt of chiffon. Year after year that's what we do in our lives, and that's worth celebrating with a day of living well at any age — and especially at fifty.

Hogan's 65th

A WALK ON THE WILD SIDE

for sixteen

They don't call them golden years for nothing! The kids are out of college, the mortgage has finally been paid off, and with any luck at all, the confetti from the retirement party has already been swept up. That's why a sixty-fifth birthday is such a great time to celebrate all the benefits of growing up by acting just a little outlandish. After years of looking out for everyone else and paying the bills, you can put all those AARP discounts to use by doing the things you always promised yourself you would do. With greater wisdom, comfort, and security, this is the time to throw the birthday party of your wildest dreams.

Of course, wildest dreams are never one-size-fits-all. One person's might involve an opulent ballroom filled with lifelong friends in formal attire. Another's might involve an intimate dinner for two at the top of the Eiffel Tower. But a client of mine named Hogan had a more literally wild dream — the kind with elephants and lions (and tigers and bears — oh my). Ever since his very first trip to the zoo as a child, he had always dreamed of going on a safari in Africa, but school, work, and raising his wonderful family had always meant more to him. So as a tribute to his years of hard work, love, and support, his wife, Betty, and their three kids and seven grandchildren pitched in to send him on one. In order to break the news with the proper fanfare — so he could share his excitement with his friends and loved ones in the tamer environment of Atlanta, Georgia — they asked me to plan a surprise celebration in their backyard. They had just one question: how could they make the exotic thrill of an African safari come alive on a quiet lawn in the suburbs? Luckily, there was a simple answer: I would stage the whole affair in one large, enclosed tent. No matter what the location, with a few of the right accessories, a tent can create the feeling of an entirely different world. For Hogan's big night, I would use native driftwood, flowers, and brush to bring inside the mysterious beauty of the great outdoors. Bright tribal masks and the sounds of the savanna would envelop guests in the embrace of a warm African night in the wilderness, while sweet, fiery spices would conjure the winds off the desert. Twinkling with candlelight and rich with the sun-baked colors of the bush, this party would bring an exhilarating piece of the fantastic adventure that awaited Hogan to the place that had always meant the most to him: home.

With greater wisdom, comfort, and security, this is the time to throw the birthday party of your wildest dreams.

Out of . . . Africa!

I LOVE WHAT A BIG WATERPROOF PARTY TENT allows me to do, but what I don't love is what a big waterproof party tent looks like. It's basically a large, white, vinyl room — not so fun to even contemplate, let alone spend hours in. I wanted Hogan and his guests to feel as though they were dining in a royal chieftain's private safari tent, not a strapped-down vinyl rental from an industrial distributor. So, when it came time to style Hogan's safari surprise party, I started at the bottom and worked my way up until the entire space appeared to be truly out of Africa.

First I covered the floor with dozens of chunky straw mats (these are inexpensive and available in the outdoor-entertaining sections of many home design stores). Then I draped yards and yards of pale, sand-colored linen across the ceiling and around the walls. I pulled big, billowing pieces of sheer beige fabric over the linen, bringing a windswept softness to the tent's interior. I trimmed the upper edges of the tent's walls with straw thatching and hung exotic "African masks" — a fun, creative job for kids to contribute to the party — and faux animal skins on the walls.

It's going to be a Wild Time!

COME CELEBRATE

Hogan's 65th

SATURDAY, OCTOBER 11, 2008

7:00 IN THE EVENING

I used the same raw burlap fabric to cover the chairs and the sides of the dining table. For the tabletop, I opted for a very chic zebra print. The clean black-and-white stripes made for an elegant juxtaposition with the surrounding rugged straw and frayed burlap edges. The lighting in a real safari tent might have involved an old British windup torch, but for this special occasion, I went a few steps further. I crafted an exotic chandelier from curly willow branches, hanging votives, and pheasant feathers. This fabulous "jungle chandelier" was suspended from the middle of the tent and spanned almost the entire length of the table. The candlelight shone through the twisted twigs, creating playful zebra stripes of light on the billowing ceiling.

HOW to Decorative tribal masks

These masks are meant to be abstract and colorful; there is no right way to make them. This is a fantastic craft project for the kids, but please have an adult handle Step 2 for safety.

MATERIALS

o inexpensive round plastic sleds

o craft paint (orange, yellow, black, and rust)

o colored raffia

o knife or small saw

o feathers

o brushes

o clear-coat spray sealant

METHOD

1. To find some images to work from, look at African art books or search the Web for African masks.

2. Using a knife or small saw, cut out eyes and a nose from a round plastic sled. Use the sled handle as the mouth (or ears) or cut your own.

3. Take a deep breath and paint your mask. Get creative!

4. Let the mask dry and spray it with clear sealant.

5. Once the mask is dry, add raffia and/or feathers.

NOTE: If you can't find a plastic sled, a plastic garbage can lid works great, too.

The table itself featured rustic metal bowls wrapped in burlap, brimming with plants such as protea and accented with exotic foliage. In among the craggy driftwood were sleek feathers and candles covered in ebony coffee beans. Amber wineglasses and tan faux-leather charger plates added a shot of warmth to each place setting. For additional textures, I used rustic flatware and rattan-patterned ceramic dinner plates. And in order to stage that final knockout touch, I created stunning napkin holders from smooth African cowrie shells and individual porcupine quills.

MATERIALS

o 1½ to 2 yards burlap material per chair (depending on the width of the fabric, this amount could be split to cover two chairs)

o hot glue and hot-glue gun

o stapler

o feathers, animal-print fabric

METHOD

1. Cut the burlap two inches wider than the chair and long enough to reach from the seat, up the chair back, and over the top of the chair back down to the floor behind it.

2. With the fabric turned inside out, drape it over the chair back, with one end touching the ground behind the chair and the other touching the seat.

3. Staple the fabric (one inch apart) along the lengths of both sides. Remove it from the chair and turn it right side out. Slip it over the back of the chair.

4. Cut a rectangular window (3 to 4 inches wide by 10 to 12 inches long) in the burlap covering the chair back.

5. Using fabric glue, attach a piece of animal-print fabric in the "window" with the back of the print facing in. Attach feathers to the top of the chair's back.

6. Fray the burlap window to create a more rustic look.

7. Place the covers over the chair backs.

NOTE: You can also accent chairs — or just the VIP chair — with curly willow branches. Simply attach the twisted branches to the top and bottom on the sides of the chair with wire.

Rugged and refined

THE COLOR SCHEME OF THIS PARTY included splashes of blazing rust, tiger yellow, and exotic zebra stripes, but for the most part I stuck to the simple "safari white." This may sound minimalist, but don't be fooled by simplicity of color when there are so many textures to consider. Juxtaposing textures can bring even the most ordinary color scheme to life. For Hogan's safari party, the contrasts were found in the pairing of decorative details. At the edges of the tent, billowing linens edged up against spiky straw thatching. Velvety faux zebra skin contrasted with rough, frayed burlap around the edges of the table and on the chair covers. Spiky porcupine quills poked through porcelain-smooth seashell napkin holders. Glossy rattan-patterned plates sat atop rugged faux leather–trimmed chargers. Rough pieces of desert driftwood lay at the base of satiny amber wineglasses. Even the invitations by Encore Studios felt rustic and masculine with layer upon layer of different textures. This invitation quite literally introduced the *feel* of the party to come. The final effect of all these textures was to add an extra dimension to all the visuals, drawing out the color and patterns and bringing guests that much closer to the special safari feeling.

A tableside adventure

ONE OF MY FAVORITE THINGS about food is that the addition of a few interesting ingredients to a familiar dish can effectively whisk you away to a foreign destination — all without luggage and security checks. Whenever the possibility of a more exotic menu arises for a birthday dinner celebration, I always remind hosts that it's absolutely crucial to respect the honoree's basic food preferences and to check for any allergies. In Hogan's case, the only thing off-limits was the ordinary, so I designed a succession of tastes that would tantalize and thrill with new sensations.

Guests began with a zinger: Ginger Island cocktails made with rum and fresh ginger roused sleeping taste buds, while Wild Pear martinis brought the soft tropical combo of pear, lemon, and lime into harmony. They then feasted on coconut-infused shrimp arrayed on a bed of spicy mixed greens and light tomato couscous, all sprinkled with toasted blanched almonds. Next, everyone dined on a traditional combination of chicken braised with olives, lemons, capers, and cumin and served over steamed rice. Following the lightly sweet, silky course of shrimp, the briny olives and tart lemon balanced each other without sacrificing a bracing sense of intrigue in the bright shift of flavors. And no birthday *bon voyage* would be complete without a little helping of good luck. To that end, the entire party sipped mint tea and shared a platter of warm benne cakes — a West African sesame cookie (*benne* means "sesame") that symbolizes good luck and is often served at Kwanzaa. For one final taste of the adventure that lay before Hogan, guests feasted on a delectable birthday cake crowned with a herd of safari animals and a tent.

the Menu

COCONUT-INFUSED SHRIMP ON A BED OF MIXED GREENS AND TOMATO COUSCOUS SPRINKLED WITH TOASTED BLANCHED ALMONDS AND DRIZZLED WITH A SPICE-COCONUT EMULSION

ORGANIC CHICKEN BREAST BRAISED WITH LEMONS, MOROCCAN OLIVES, CAPERS, AND CUMIN OVER STEAMED RICE

ASSORTMENT OF BENNE CAKES AND MINT TEA

AFRICAN SAFARI CARROT CAKE

Ginger island

2 ounces BACARDI® Superior Rum

1 ounce fresh lime juice

1 tablespoon sugar

1 slice fresh ginger

club soda

apricot slice skewered with fresh mint, as garnish

MUDDLE the ginger, sugar, and lime juice in a
cocktail shaker with a spoon. Add the rum and ice
and shake well. Strain into a low-ball glass with
ice. Garnish with the apricot and mint.

Wild pear cocktail

2 ounces BACARDI® Limon

1 ounce strained lemonade

splash of fresh lime juice

3 or 4 ounces sparkling pear juice

pear slice cored and cut into a ring and dipped in
raw sugar, as garnish

IN a goblet with ice, add the rum, lemonade, and
lime juice. Stir well and top with chilled sparkling
pear juice. Garnish with a pear slice dipped in
sugar.

Rugged and spicy

WHENEVER I DESIGN A SEND-OFF PARTY of any kind, I like to bring the sights and sounds of the honoree's destination into the space of the party. But the smell is a different thing. At Hogan's safari send-off, for example, aromatic realism was out of the question — nothing kills a party like the musk on a herd of muddy elephants. So instead, I opted for a more romantic interpretation of the air off the desert at night. Though I generally try to avoid using heavily scented candles for a dinner party — particularly in an enclosed space, like a tent — mixing the votives in the chandelier with just a couple of mild sandalwood and cinnamon candles left a warm, natural fragrance hovering just above the space of the table. Subtlety is essential here, so if you're planning to pick scented candles for your own dinner party, I strongly recommend testing them to make sure they aren't too overpowering — you don't want to leave your guests longing for the perfume of the elephants instead. At Hogan's party it was little touches like this one that swept guests away to another land, however fancifully imagined. As the trail of smoke from the candles mingled in the air with the aromas of leather, coffee beans, and the bright, peppery spices of the meal, a harmony was achieved that was both inviting and unfamiliar. With each course served, a different variation wafted up into the air, a constant awakening of each guest's senses to new experiences.

Jungle boogie

I ALWAYS USE MUSIC to transport guests mentally from one place to another. A simple Latin beat can trigger the craving for a Mojito cocktail and make the day's business fade from the mind almost instantly; a few bars of the Beach Boys and a summer barbecue starts to really cook. Music will "take you there" every time. For this safari surprise party, I wanted to take Hogan and his guests deep into the jungle. To accomplish this, I turned to various nature sanctuary sound tracks, which, though often overlooked when it comes to entertaining, can provide a wonderful theatrical backdrop to cocktail party chatter. As soon as Hogan's guests arrived, they were lured into the tent by the intriguing distant sounds of gently cooing monkeys, fluting birds, and braying zebras. As they mingled over cocktails, their conversation was punctuated now and then by the sound of a trumpeting elephant or hissing cheetah. They all felt like they had taken a trip not to someone's suburban home but halfway across the globe to sub-Saharan Africa.

Once the guests were situated in a true *Animal Planet* mind-set, I switched gears to an upbeat Swahili rumba. A few compilations of African music later and all the guests were tapping their feet and shimmying in their seats. Most African music is lively, cheerful, and pleasing to all age groups. If you purchase World Music that you're unfamiliar with, though, listen to it before the party to make sure it will be appropriate.

- Clear tents should not be used in the hot summer months. They look stunning when the weather is cooler, but they can act as a solarium and create uncomfortable and even unsafe hot temperatures in the blazing heat of midsummer.

- Always have a rain plan when you're entertaining using a tent. Meet with your tent company to map out exactly what will happen if it rains (i.e., you may need a tent with walls). The rule of thumb is that if there is a 30 percent or higher chance of rain, you should put your rain plan into action. Also, ask your tent company when the last moment is that they can come and install the tent. Typically, a rain plan needs to go into action about three days prior to the party date.

- It's important that your table be at least four feet wide so that you can fit twelve-inch charger plates on both sides, with room for glasses and a dynamic floral display down the middle. One long four-by-eight-foot table can host a total of ten guests comfortably.

- Tents are wonderful for parties: They provide shelter from the elements and extra space when an interior seems too small for a big party. They can also provide a nice interior space for an outdoor party while keeping your house private.

- I always express to my clients that tent transformation is a must. I let them know, though, that this can become costly. In fact, throwing a tent party can be the most expensive way to entertain.

- When you are hosting a dinner party, it is important to serve each course quickly so that your guests do not feel trapped at the table. You want to keep them wanting more rather than wishing the party would end sooner. A rule of thumb: each course should be served, eaten, and cleared within thirty minutes.

- Flooring is a key element when you're giving a tented party. Whether you get a subfloor built or Astroturf or a porta-floor laid, a floor is key to keeping the ground dry in bad weather and is more comfortable for guests, too . . . especially those in high heels.

- Depending on the size of your party, you may want to have rented bathrooms brought in. Many companies provide very nice ones, and having them available will keep your house from being overrun. If you are relying on your own bathrooms and have a septic system, make sure it was cleaned recently so that you can avoid any mishaps.

- When entertaining in a tent on a very hot night, consider passing around trays of iced, lemon-scented towelettes. You can buy presoaked frozen towelettes and have your caterer pass them around so that your guests can cool off after a long dance set.

- If you are planning on draping your tent with fabric, check with your tent and lighting company to see if they can provide fabric for you.

Last night I dreamed I was in Africa . . .

AS THE NIGHT WORE ON at Hogan's party, the shadows that were cast against the top and sides of the tent grew bolder and more animated in the twinkling firelight of the hanging votives. Profiles of faces nodding in excitement, the dramatic, tangled branches of the chandelier, and glowing amber glasses raised in celebration could all be seen. Against the pleasant hum of tall tales and warm laughter, it was like a miniature magic lantern show of one great evening with Hogan's own gregarious little tribe. Perhaps the best part of the entire evening, though, was watching Hogan share his excitement about the trip with all the loved ones who had made it possible. As he unwrapped binoculars, sun hats, and hiking boots from well-wishing friends, his passion became theirs, too. We do not all dream so wildly (personally, my own plans for a sixty-fifth birthday will not include the possibility of fleeing from a pack of cheetahs in an open Jeep). But one of the most wonderful things a passionately imagined birthday party can do is create a space where we can share, if only briefly, just a little piece of the dreams we hold in our heart of hearts. The fantastic adventure Hogan had spent his whole life imagining still lay ahead of him in a distant land, but I could tell that another one, just as treasured, was already taking place that evening on a not-so-quiet suburban lawn.

Gloria's 75th

AN EVENING UNDER THE APPLE TREES

for twenty-four

When it comes right down to it, a good birthday party is all about enjoying life to the fullest in the present moment. That's why a lot of people assume that teenagers make the ideal partygoers — bungee jumping off cliffs and entering swimsuit contests for MTV's spring break specials are activities reserved for folks who know how to *carpe diem*, if you know what I mean. But there's a difference between seizing the day and savoring it, and after years of planning birthday parties for people of all ages, I've realized that it's the seventy-somethings who know how to savor it best of all. With a little more experience under their belts, they take true pleasure in the sight of a flower in full bloom, a rare bird, or a smiling grandchild — no bungee cords necessary. In short, they know how to enjoy a party because they know how to enjoy life. So whenever I get the chance to design a seventy-fifth birthday party, I seldom look to the past or the future for my inspiration. Instead, I look for it in the present moment of the honoree's life and try to accentuate all the vibrant living things that make each day new for him or her.

When I visited a client of mine named Patsy to discuss plans for her sister Gloria's seventy-fifth birthday party, that inspiration appeared right before my eyes — literally. I was walking through the apple orchard she'd just bought with her husband while she told me about Gloria's immediate love for the place and her recent experiments with different apple pie recipes. Then, just as the sun set on the horizon, a bright green apple, fully ripened by the sun, dropped from above to my feet. I picked it up, took a bite, and started planning a sumptuous outdoor dinner party that would make the most of the enchanting evening light, the tree-lined, gently rolling hills, and the delicious fruits of the orchard. Candlelit farmhouse tables decked with formal place settings would line the wide paths between trees twinkling with votives, integrating guests into the lush, homey landscape without sacrificing the majestic view of the sky above. Colors of bright apple green and pure white would add the snappy floral character of a perfect Granny Smith to patterned linens, stately lampshades, and long ribbons streaming down from the trees. Gorgeous teak chairs and benches would encircle the tables, while ivy topiaries trimmed like apple tree tops, antique iron candelabras, and sparkling new decanters of crisp apple wine would serve as table runners — fresh reminders of the raw materials that make life so sweet. It would be a special night for Gloria, made so almost entirely by the affection of her sister and the exquisite experience of seeing the everyday anew in its living beauty.

After years of planning birthday parties for people of all ages, I've realized that it's the seventy-somethings who know how to savor life best of all.

The apple of my eye

I WANTED THIS PARTY to look as if an elegant country dining room had fallen from above and landed perfectly centered between two rows of apple trees. How hard could that be? I just needed a few hours, a couple of forklifts (maybe a truck), and an elegant country dining room with no plans for Saturday night! As I set out to make this dream a reality, I could only imagine one thing: the look on Gloria's face as she took that first step out from between the apple trees to find her family and friends gathered in the amber glow of a late-afternoon sunset, glasses raised and smiles beaming.

As the guests entered the orchard, they were greeted by an apple tree simply blooming . . . with escort cards. Using wooden clothespins, I had fastened vintage seed packets and handwritten escort cards to long satin ribbons that were dangling from the branches. A few bushels of green apples piled at the foot of the trunk made for a springtime

Christmas-tree effect. Although they would hardly be noticeable at first, I attached dozens and dozens of hanging lanterns and votives to the branches of trees all the way up and down the orchard. Around a wide, deep natural-wicker sofa set off from the dining area (a real kick-off-your-shoes retreat for after-dinner drinks) I placed elegant antique candelabras on the ground, looking almost as if they were lying there awaiting installation. (A few calculatedly "unfinished" gestures like this always help guests feel like they can loosen up.) After the sun set, the candles in them started to flicker a warm golden light throughout the whole orchard.

The big event itself was situated right amid the trees, where three whitewashed tables were set lengthwise between them. Rather than using matching chairs, I opted for a casual combination of long teak wooden benches and chairs. The entire setting echoed the natural colors of the orchard, from apple green and golden yellow to natural wood and crisp country white. The runner, napkins, and candelabra lampshades were all made from matching delicate green-and-white embroidered fabric. Along the length of the runner and surrounding the base of the antique iron candelabras, I arranged a romantic composition of fluttery maidenhair ferns and tangled ivy topiaries. Pale green votive holders were nestled among an eclectic mix of stunning Saint-Louis crystal wineglasses. (As long as they're beautiful and they match the general look of the party, it doesn't matter if you mix and match the drinking glasses.) Elegant decanters of golden apple chardonnay and simple glass jugs of lemon water were placed within arm's length of each place setting. I chose Marc Blackwell's Eric's Time china for its unique pattern of gold and silver clock faces and Lenox's Gorham Chantilly Gold flatware for its antique charm. Finally, a single jade-green rose head was propped up against each place card and folded napkin.

HOW to Whitewashed farm tables

For Gloria's party we took three old farm tables that were pretty beaten up and brought them back to life with a little layered sponge painting. This simple process can help you revive old outdoor furniture.

MATERIALS

- wood table (old or new)
- light green latex outdoor paint
- off-white latex outdoor paint
- natural sea sponge
- cotton cloth
- latex gloves
- empty coffee can (for paint)
- semigloss outdoor clear-coat sealant

METHOD

1. Clean or lightly sand the table to remove wax, dirt, polish, and so on. Wear gloves to protect your hands.

2. Mix ⅔ green paint to ⅓ water in a coffee can. (The paint will be slightly runny.)

3. Lightly sponge the paint onto the table, using enough to cover the entire thing while allowing a little of the natural grain to show through. Lightly rub off excess paint.

4. Once the paint is dry, repeat the process with the off-white paint and let it dry for about ten minutes (depending on the temperature). Wipe off any excess paint with a cotton cloth to achieve the desired washed look.

5. Apply a semigloss outdoor clear-coat sealant.

HOW to Escort cards in the apple tree

MATERIALS

- card stock (one 8½ x 11-inch sheet will do one or two seed packets)
- paper or fabric to cover the card stock
- scissors
- vintage seed packets (as many as you have guests or couples; available online or at some garden supply stores)
- ribbon
- hot glue and hot-glue gun
- paint pen or marker
- escort cards with a border
- wood clothespins

METHOD

1. Cut the card stock so that it's slightly larger than your seed packets (most will be about the size of an index card).

2. Cover the card stock with a unique fabric or paper that matches your color scheme and overall design. Use hot glue to mount the fabric or paper, making sure to cover the entire back and overlap all edges by one inch on the front.

3. Glue the seed packet to the front, hiding all rough edges.

4. Tie ribbons to tree branches at various heights.

5. Write each guest's or couple's name on an escort card with a paint pen or marker. Write the corresponding table number on the back of the card.

6. Using a wooden clothespin, attach each escort card to a seed packet.

7. Attach the seed packet escort cards to the dangling ribbons. You can attach one or more to each ribbon.

NOTE: These cards work well for intimate or smaller parties.

Barefoot in the orchard

PERHAPS IT'S BECAUSE I SPEND SO MUCH TIME in the city, but when I find myself out in the country or even the suburbs, I just want to kick my shoes off. The feel of cool grass between my toes gives me that special feeling ("Toto, we're not in Chelsea anymore . . ."). Even though, technically speaking, there is dirt in nature's own carpet, it just doesn't seem dirty when it's in a place like Patsy's country orchard. I wanted each delicate texture of her orchard to play a role in mentally transporting Gloria and her guests to another place, where shoes were optional and time was not an issue. The tangled but pert ivy topiaries echoed the rustling leaves and branches of the surrounding apple trees, while the ferns were as soft as the new spring grass underfoot. The delicate surface of the embroidered linens suggested tea towels and pretty aprons from country kitchens of the past. At the same time, the smooth votive holders on the table were as glossy and green as a fresh Granny Smith. Sleek crystal glasses were in pure harmony with the glistening drops from the afternoon sprinklers. Finally, when dessert was served, the rich, flaky texture of apple pie pastry brought the whole outdoor room together.

A is for apple

SAVORING FOOD IS A LOT LIKE SAVORING LIFE: when the basic ingredients are truly great, the pure, natural character of each flavor shines through and you don't need much else. Well, it didn't take long to see that Gloria and her family had already thought to combine the best possible ingredients of both into one. They found the apple orchard brimming with ripe fruit just beyond Patsy's backyard not only a pleasure to tend and a pleasure to look at but also a joy to cook with when harvest time rolled around. In order to pay tribute to the bounty of fruit that grows there — not to mention Gloria's passion for it — I asked Jeremy Griffiths, one of the wonderful chefs I work with, to design a homey menu that showcased it with clarity and simplicity.

the Menu

HEIRLOOM TOMATO SALAD WITH MÂCHE, PARMIGIANO-REGGIANO, AND AGED BALSAMIC DRESSING

ROAST ORGANIC CHICKEN BREAST WITH CARAMELIZED APPLES AND POTATOES, VEGETABLE COUSCOUS, AND HICKORY SAUCE

INDIVIDUAL APPLE PIES FROM THE LITTLE PIE COMPANY WITH BLACKBERRY COULIS

THREE-TIER SIGNATURE MEGÈVE CAKE

And he set out to do just that. But when he discovered a patch of heirloom tomatoes growing in Patsy's kitchen garden behind the house, he could not resist using them, too, and in the end, his instincts were flawless. The firm, juicy tomatoes laid a slightly sweet base for a salad of tender, floral mâche, salty Parmigiano-Reggiano, and aged balsamic vinaigrette. And its subtle sweet-tart flavors set just the right tone for the main course to follow, which paired roast chicken breast with an earthy compote of sugar-kissed caramelized apples and potatoes and a smattering of vegetable couscous with a smoky hint of hickory. Carafes of chilled apple chardonnay placed up and down the table pulled it all together with crisp, cool panache. Like a chord strummed on a guitar with perfect clarity, every tone and note on the plate sang together in the key of the humble apple, and it was all the lovelier for it.

When the dessert course finally arrived, guests were treated to an altogether different homage to the orchard where they dined. First, a steaming apple pie perfumed with bright lemon and served with a lush, dark dollop of blackberry coulis arrived so that guests could share a bite of heaven from a famous specialty pie company. But for the regal touch of luxury that a seventy-fifth birthday demands, I had Florian Bellanger of the world-famous fine-foods emporium Fauchon in New York City customize their signature Megève cake for an evening on the apple farm. The smooth, fragrant Tahitian vanilla that flavors this unforgettable cake remained exactly as usual, but in place of the dark chocolate ganache that normally covers it, Bellanger laid the palest green icing and dotted each tier with spectacular, glistening apples sculpted from blown sugar.

the SCENT

Apple-kissed

THE SHARP, FRESH SCENT of a crisp apple makes everyone smile. It's appetizing, refreshing, and even makes us a little nostalgic. And where better to enjoy that fresh aroma we all love than in the apple orchard itself? Among the rows of small, fruit-laden trees, there was nothing to breathe in but the fresh fragrances of a natural country paradise. Patsy taught me a few things about orchards and aromas. Ungathered fallen apples eventually start to ferment, producing a pungent and extra-sweet aroma (not to mention the odd drunk bird, apple juice still fresh on its beak). Patsy's springtime orchard was free of any funky fermenting fumes, so all I had to do was focus on amplifying the fresh ones. I started by placing bushels of McIntosh apples around the party area, then upped the aromatic ante with a menu of slivered, sliced, and stewed apples. Finally, I decanted some delicious locally made apple wine. Hints of apple sweetness drifted around the dining tables, invisibly conducting magic all through the night. I also introduced one tiny and subtle hint of femininity into this pretty setting by placing a single jade-green rose head in front of each place setting. These little buds conjured up just a touch more of that invisible natural magic to carry the guests long into a dreamy night beneath the stars.

Hoot, hoot

I KNOW THE WORD "PLANNER" IS IN MY JOB TITLE, but I can always count on a few perfect party moments that even I could not have planned for in advance. These often involve impromptu concerts. It turns out Gloria's friends and family are quite the multilingual set — at least when it comes to the lyrics of "Happy Birthday." Right there under the stars Gloria was treated to the classic birthday serenade in English, Italian, German, French, and even Serbian! Then, Gloria's brother-in-law Misha stood up and performed a stunning and exotic a cappella version of "Happy Birthday" in Russian. It was so beautiful that everyone got choked up. And then, as if on cue, a second magical concert began: the bizarre hootings of a couple of resident owls.

Spring and summer outdoor dinner parties often do not require much in the way of planned music. This is especially true when the natural setting is secluded. The music of night owls, tree frogs, or even crickets can be exciting to a group of guests whose days are typically spent surrounded by the sounds of car radios, cell phones, and the five-o'clock news. After the owls had finished their little conversation, Gloria hooted back at them and then the whole table joined in. These dinner-party guests could all hoot as loudly as they wanted, and for a moment they all felt as silly and free as kids around a campfire.

TUTERA tips

○ Be sure to wait until after sunset to light any outdoor candles that are not enclosed in glass. The wind usually calms down once the sun has set.

○ When using fresh fruits as decor, buy them in bulk (perhaps at your local farmer's market) and have empty baskets or bags so your guests can take them home as an additional sweet memory of the party.

○ When baking apples, peel a one-inch band around the top to avoid cracking while baking.

○ Leftover fabric is great for covering or accenting a lampshade, napkin, or even a table runner — you can glue it or sew it or even use iron-on tape.

○ A topiary or other plant as your centerpiece not only looks great but it lasts. You can take it home and enjoy a lasting memory of the party.

○ The best way to keep outdoor teak furniture looking great is to clean and oil each piece in the spring and then clean and cover them for the fall and winter months. This will keep them beautiful and durable for years to come.

○ Maidenhair ferns are delicate and prefer an environment with a stable temperature and humidity level. Place them in a well-lit sunroom or on a sunny windowsill and keep them moist, but don't overwater them. A mister can help to keep them beautiful.

○ If you can't find organic produce, soak your produce in cool water with lemon juice and salt to remove pesticides. Rinse and dry it before cooking or eating it.

○ When hosting a casual outdoor party, encourage your guests to get comfortable by setting up a lounge area. You can even bring out a couch, chairs, and throw pillows to create a relaxing spot in the grass.

○ Don't be afraid to use your good crystal and china for parties — and to mix and match patterns and create your own style. Remember, if you keep it in your cabinets, it's just going to waste!

An apple (and a party) a day . . .

IN ALL OF OUR MEETINGS before the evening of the party, Patsy and I talked about how beautiful the dinner hour would be with the colors of the sunset melting in the sky over the orchard. We had it all timed and down to a science — or so we thought. However, on the night of the party, the moon seemed to rise in the sky just a little more quickly than we'd expected, and before we knew it, our bright outpost of flickering candles, laughter, and clinking crystal sat in the middle of a dark field. I cannot deny that at first I felt a deep sense of disappointment as I imagined what Patsy might be thinking about all of our dashed plans. I quickly realized how foolish that was, though. At the end of the table, the two sisters were leaning together in the warm light of the candles, looking up at the bright silver moon, and wondering what good luck could have brought this full, perfect moon to them at such an early hour. The guests all sat enjoying the cool night breeze for hours on end before they made their way to their cars, laden with packets of seeds for the garden and bushels of just-picked apples, their arms looped through the arms of their loved ones.

"To love and to be loved is the greatest happiness of existence."

Menu

Seared sea scallops over baby spinach
Creme fraiche and sweet chile dressing

Baby arugula with warm mushroom
Vinaigrette

Roasted cod with citrus vinaigrette and
grilled asparagus

Chocolate polenta cake and roasted
strawberries

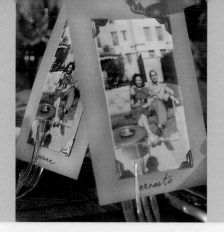

Jo Ann and Joe's 100th

A HEARTH-WARMING DINNER

for sixteen

There are few events as exceptional as a one hundredth birthday. You can squeeze a pretty stunning collection of experiences, memories, friends, and accomplishments into the space of a century, and it can be daunting to plan a celebration for the fascinating people who know this firsthand. If nothing else, think of all the fabulous parties they must have attended. If my own experience has taught me anything, it's that the best way to celebrate such a rich life is to amplify the simple little pleasures that made it a happy one first, and then, day by day, a long one.

Now, by any account Joe and Jo Ann, the two honorees of this double-centennial dinner party for sixteen, are pretty exceptional in their own right. Not just because they were born only a few days apart in the same town with almost identical names (it was in the stars!), but because they've traveled the world, worked as teachers, and raised a family over an unbelievable eighty-one years of marriage. I thought it would be hard to refrain from making epic gestures as they reached this incredible birthday milestone together, but after hearing countless stories from their children and grandchildren about "Fred and Ginger with spatulas," and after finding them tending a simmering pot on the stove in their kitchen more than once, it became clear that Joe and Jo Ann savored life most just after they'd adjusted it with seasonings. That's when this intimate dinner for Joe, Jo Ann, and the people they love to cook for most — their immediate family and close friends — began to take shape. Just as the ordinary ritual of preparing a meal with love had made their lives together extraordinary, this party would transform the everyday inventory of the kitchen into the finery of a grand centennial celebration. The cheerful citrus yellow, green, and orange color palette of the couple's own cherished kitchen would set an invigorating but elegant tone for an evening by the family hearth. Staples from the pantry and refrigerator would harmonize with flowers from the window box in a centerpiece that looked good enough to eat, and Jo Ann's collection of rummage-sale silverware, vintage copper cookery, and treasured family photographs would put an unexpected personal accent on the traditional accessories of the formal dining room. All in all, this birthday ode to a lifetime of laughter and cooking would make the perfect recipe for an unforgettable family affair.

> All in all, this birthday ode to a lifetime of laughter and cooking would make the perfect recipe for an unforgettable family affair.

From pantry to party

ARMED WITH A FEW WOODEN SPOONS and a dream, I set out to create the life of this party from the look of the pantry. You'd be surprised how much elegance can be eked out of a well-seasoned stockpot, a few dozen old forks, and a basket of colorful citrus fruit. Instead of the usual balloons or streamers, Joe and Jo Ann's birthday party featured two funky "cook's chandeliers" made from an eclectic assortment of kitchen utensils (from spatulas to sauté pans) and candlelit votives and suspended by iron pot racks. The flickering candlelight bounced off the dangling metal objects, causing a subtle sparkle of light over the table. Below, on two square dining tables, a little metallic shimmer came from the pewter gravy boats brimming with daises, hydrangeas, and viburnum. Hints of pewter were also found around the edges of cheese board charger plates, along the rims of the plates, up the stems of crystal glasses, and framing romantic black-and-white photos of the birthday couple. The cocktail

Jo Ann
100th
Joseph

So many sunrises witnessed...
So many sips of wine aged to perfection...
Please join JoAnn and Joseph Capadano
as they celebrate 100 years of life
on Saturday, the sixth of August
Two thousand and eight
at one o'clock in the afternoon

tables got their share of heavy metal, too, in the form of striking candelabras crafted from rummage-sale silverware. Even the place-card holders
were fashioned from the twisted tines of old forks. To complement the
baroque silverware place settings and creative kitchen candelabras and
create a casual family feeling, I gathered an eclectic mix of chairs from
other rooms in the house.

As for the color scheme, a buttery yellow set a warm mood, while
touches of lime green and clementine orange added a cheerful flair. These
citrus hues were woven throughout the plaid silk runners, tablecloths,
napkins, ribbons, candles, place cards, and menus — and even the icing
on the cake. Dozens of robust lemons, limes, and clementines spilled out
over the table, around the cake, and on the mantel. The whole room

HOW to Floral breads

MATERIALS

○ bread (any size, any
shape), unsliced

○ serrated knife

○ Oasis floral foam (1 block
per loaf of bread)

○ plastic (grocery bag
works well)

○ flowers of your choice

○ water

○ sheet moss, available at
floral shops (optional)

METHOD

1. Soak the Oasis in water
until it is completely saturated.

2. With a serrated knife, cut
into the center of the

bread to make an opening
that will act as a vase for
the flowers. Remove the
bread from the opening.
(Save it for bread pudding,
croutons, or bread crumbs.)
Keep the bottom of the loaf
intact.

3. Line the opening in the
bread with plastic to keep
the Oasis from soaking the
bread.

4. Cut the Oasis to fit inside
the hollowed-out bread and
insert it.

5. Arrange the flowers as you
wish, starting in the center
and working toward the
edges, making sure to cover
the Oasis. Use a bit of moss
to cover, if needed.

Dried-bean votives

MATERIALS

- a variety of pretty, colorful dried beans and/or seeds
- paper plate
- simple glass votive candleholders
- high-temp hot glue and hot-glue gun
- candle insert

METHOD

1. Mix a variety of dried beans together on a paper plate.

2. Apply hot glue to the votive candleholder, top to bottom, covering a quarter of the candleholder at a time.

3. Roll the glue-covered holder over the beans to cover it. Repeat until covered.

4. Place a wax candle in the candleholder.

NOTE: This technique works for covering napkin rings, too. Cut a paper-towel roll into two-inch sections.

glowed as if basking in the morning sun. The plates (by Match) were ablaze in deep orange. I even came up with a striking citrus cocktail.

The final decorative "Tutera Touch" came in the form of an ode to Joe's famous homemade Italian minestrone. I created a mouthwatering bouquet of leeks, flat-leaf parsley, onions, dried pasta, and baguettes and arranged it in a large stockpot in the center of the dining table. Around the base of this savory still life, pale green pillar candles rose up from tall mason jars filled with assorted dried beans. Interspersed between the candles, gorgeous daffodils, anemones, and soft viburnum burst from the edges of carved-out ciabatta loaves. The napkin rings were covered with a mosaic of red and brown dried beans. Over the whole scene bean-covered votive candleholders cast an amber glow.

Individual menus included a love quote to remind guests how food, fun, and love have long been intertwined for Joe and Jo Ann. Attached to their parting favor (a personalized apron and jar of green, yellow, and orange M&M's) was a final heartwarming message: "It's not so much about what's on the table that matters . . . as what's in the chairs."

Personalized photo-menu cards

This method can be used to create custom place cards, too.

MATERIALS

- ○ color-copied photos
- ○ photo-adhering corners
- ○ card stock (any color)
- ○ photo-safe glue or double-stick tape
- ○ ribbon
- ○ hole punch
- ○ fine-point marker or calligraphy pen

METHOD

1. Cut the card stock to the desired size for menu cards.

2. Cut the copied photos to fit on the card stock, leaving room at the top for a ribbon as well as enough space to write the menu below.

3. Stick the copied photo in place with the photo corners.

4. Write the menu below the photo.

5. Punch two holes at the top to add an additional accent of a ribbon bow.

Things that last

JUST AS JOE AND JO ANN REMAINED ANCHORED to each other, I wanted this party to feel robust, hearty, and sturdy on its feet. Instead of lace and delicate china, I opted for weightier decorative objects — things that last. Elegant wooden cutting boards grounded each place setting. The textures of pewter, crystal, and copper as well as weighted jars of beans and M&M's all added to a sense of weightiness befitting the occasion. Crisscrossed at each table corner, wooden spoons added a constructive element to an otherwise whimsical kick-pleated tablecloth. The heavy stockpot — brimming with staples from the farmer's market — served as a reminder of Joe and Jo Ann's many days in the kitchen, often spent cooking big Sunday dinners. Some of the home-style decorations had a glamour all to themselves: the dried beans on each napkin ring felt like smooth precious stones, and the scattered citrus fruits were like dazzling springtime ornaments. To soften the edges of the metallic surfaces, I opted for lots of small fluttery bouquets of daisies, daffodils, hydrangeas, and viburnum. A contrast in textures is always crucial; here I found it by pairing delicate flowers with rustic loaves, shimmering metal surfaces with smooth beans, and crisp silk table linens with the curvy soft edges of wooden spoons. From now on, every time a member of the family flips a pancake with a wide, flexible spatula, they'll remember this wonderful day spent with Joe and Jo Ann.

It don't mean a thing if it ain't got that zing

THE CITRUS COLOR SCHEME of Joe and Jo Ann's cheerful kitchen played a big role in inspiring the sprightly accents for the decor of this classic dinner party, and it also influenced greatly the spirit of the menu. From the first time I met them, I knew this discriminating couple had a zest for life, so light, simple, and refreshing flavors with a natural zing fit the bill for their fete just perfectly. It all started with the timeless elegance of the cocktail hour. One of my favorite things about working with older clients is that they *all* properly revere this ceremonious first step of the dining experience. I rose to the occasion by offering a custom-made citrus martini kissed with fresh lemonade and garnished with tiny slices of clementine and lime. The accompanying hors d'oeuvres of cool sliced cucumber topped with a smoked salmon salad and assorted crostini offered a light, fanciful taste of the delicacies to come.

The first course treated guests to tender and sweet seared sea scallops over baby spinach, which tantalized with just a touch of crème fraîche and sweet chili dressing. Next came a spicy arugula salad tamed only by a warm vinaigrette of mushrooms and tomatoes. For the main

course, Joe, Jo Ann, and their guests savored the gentle texture of roasted cod finished with a tangy citrus relish and a few prim spears of grilled asparagus. And for dessert, a fragrant pile of roasted strawberries brought a little taste of the garden to every luscious bite of chocolate polenta cake. But take my word for it: guests who saved room for the one-of-a-kind birthday cake went home extra-full. There was no resisting the breathtaking custom cake from Cakediva bakery, which was meticulously designed to remind everyone of the enormous baskets of fresh vegetables Joe always brought home from the local farmer's market. With carefully handcrafted icing that evoked the weave of the basket and the plaid cloth he used for a liner (which also inspired the fabric for the tablecloths), it was a feast for the taste buds as well as the eyes. Like every other dish that graced the table of these food lovers' one hundredth birthday, it refreshed the senses for all the happy returns to come.

the Menu

SEARED SEA SCALLOPS OVER BABY SPINACH WITH CRÈME FRAÎCHE AND SWEET CHILI DRESSING

BABY ARUGULA WITH WARM MUSHROOM AND TOMATO VINAIGRETTE

ROASTED COD WITH CITRUS RELISH AND GRILLED ASPARAGUS

CHOCOLATE POLENTA CAKE AND ROASTED STRAWBERRIES WITH SWEET CREAM

VEGETABLE-BASKET CAKE

Citrus martini

2 ounces Belvedere vodka

1 ounce strained lemonade

½ ounce strained clementine juice

splash of fresh lime juice

1 wedge each of lime and clementine, for garnish

COMBINE the first four ingredients in a cocktail shaker filled with ice. Swirl gently and pour into glasses. Garnish with lime and clementine slices.

Citrus joy!

THERE'S A REASON one lemon-scented dishwashing detergent is called Joy. Lemon has a reputation for its perky, mood-lifting fragrance. In the language of aromatherapy, citrus is an energy giver. You might call it the Prozac of fragrances. For this mellow (and yellow) family birthday dinner, it was important to keep the energy upbeat in a smooth and subtle way. So I enlisted a few punchy citrus scents to work their invisible, stimulating effect throughout the evening. Guests got their first charge from the lemon, lime, and clementine cocktail. Then, when the guests were seated, the tart fragrance of decorative citrus fruits helped maintain the upbeat energy. A sweet citrus vinaigrette kept the ball rolling throughout the meal, and, for the finale, the birthday candles (inserted into fruits instead of the cake) set off a whole new citrus-aroma explosion.

Another set of explosive aromas came pouring from the swinging kitchen door as the first course was served. The sizzle of freshly seared scallops with a hint of garlic and wine made mouths water in anticipation of the savory family meal to come. The centerpiece (a virtual vegetable patch) spruced the energy of the room with hints of leafy green freshness and the waft of warm home-baked bread.

Memories

SOME BIRTHDAY PARTIES DON'T REQUIRE A LOT OF MUSIC. In fact, at a momentous occasion such as this, the focus is really on the birthday toasts and, more important, what the honorees have to say. After all, they've got one hundred years of stories to tell — and enough accumulated wisdom between them to help every great-grandkid through college. Music played at a very low volume during cocktails and dinner. After dessert, however, the younger kids in the family unveiled a new turntable that they had bought so that Joe and Jo Ann could dust off a few old records and get a little sentimental. It turned out that their "hi-fi" had been broken since 1971, so they were thrilled. We played a few Scott Joplin records to get the memories going, and then turned down the volume and let Jo Ann and Joe riff! They told stories for hours, regaling everyone with hilarious tales from Joe's first job as an errand boy for rich Wall Street bankers just before the big crash and about the time he tried to win Jo Ann with a bouquet of wilted tulips picked from a median strip on Park Avenue. Sometimes a little dinner conversation is all it takes to make music for everyone's ears.

TUTERA tips

○ A lemon zester is the best tool for removing only the outer zest and fragrant oils of citrus fruits. A grater sometimes takes off some of the bitter pith, too.

○ Personalized favors are a wonderful final touch for any party. Create small, sweet favors using M&M's in colors to match the look of your party. You can even personalize them at www.mms.com.

○ When using fabric paint, read the instructions carefully. Most need to be heat set (with an iron) to cure the paint and make it washable. This will ensure years of use and is especially important for an item such as an apron that is intended for lots of messy wear and tear!

○ For a more personal touch, add a favorite quote (from a famous person, or one of your own) to one or more of the various custom paper goods: invitations, menu cards, cocktail napkins, place cards, gift bags, and so on. This will not add to your costs, but it will add a little something for your guests to talk about. You can find famous thematic quotes online or in books of quotations.

○ For a momentous occasion, create a video montage of the guest of honor's life. You can hire a videographer to compile video footage combined with photo images to create a memory of a lifetime for the party and for years to come.

○ Create a simple runner for your table by attaching place mats to one another (sew them together or use no-sew iron-on tape to connect them). You can also use laminated old photos as place mats or — when linked together — a runner.

○ To make serving cocktails a cinch, premix them in pitchers and chill them in the refrigerator. Be sure to cover the pitchers with plastic wrap to keep the drinks fresh. When ready to serve, simply shake the drinks over ice in a cocktail shaker, as you would normally. You can also keep pitchers of cocktails chilled by filling a Ziploc bag with ice and placing it in the pitcher — it will chill the drink without diluting it.

○ Make your own citrus-infused olive oil. Simply place two or three tablespoons of fresh zest (lemon or orange zest works best) in a bottle of olive oil. Shake well and wait at least twenty-four hours before using.

○ When making your own salad dressing, substitute fresh lime juice for the vinegar. This adds a fresh and light flavor to any salad.

○ Ask your caterer to provide (or purchase them yourself) small, colorful gift boxes and ribbon or twine to box up individual slices of the cake. This way, your guests can take home any leftover cake and have "sweet dreams" of the party.

Hundreds of smiles

I MUST ADMIT that before that evening with Joe, Jo Ann, and their amazing family, I'd never even considered the logistics of one hundred birthday candles. But the look on their faces when the cake was unveiled was not the only highlight of the night for me. At the end of the party, after the last family story had been told, the dishes had been cleared, and the dancing was done, I offered to help Joe and Jo Ann distribute a few special gifts of remembrance to their guests. Along with a classic pewter-and-glass canister of M&M's matching the color palette of the party — which came complete with a handwritten note bearing Jo Ann's most valued wisdom on entertaining — everyone received a personalized apron with the saying "Too Many Cooks in the Kitchen." I was surprised at first when Joe refused my help. But my surprise turned to delight when he turned to me and said, "You sit down, because I'm just getting started — this was the party of the century!"

Conclusion

In the past, whenever I heard someone offer birthday wishes "with many happy returns," I understood the saying in its most basic sense — as a kind of advance on all the birthday wishes that lay ahead in the years to come. But in the course of planning the parties described in this book and assembling them here for an even wider audience, I started to think of the phrase in other ways, too. For instance, I've always considered parties a kind of gift, and in this sense, the happy returns that come from a thoroughly celebrated birthday ripple out to all the people who are present to enjoy it. I was lucky enough to join Gloria and her sister Patsy on that evening beneath the stars in the apple orchard, and all of a sudden, I felt like I was the one getting the gift: sharing a wondrous evening with a couple of amazing women I now call friends. It's as if the very act of sharing that birthday parties occasion provides a happy return of another kind altogether. The idea of the happy return has become especially meaningful to me as I've been planning for a milestone birthday of my own: a weekend of parties in Tuscany to celebrate my fortieth. Every step of the way, the clients who have learned of my upcoming birthday have offered thoughtful ideas, recommended out-of-the-way restaurants, and wished me well. I know that participating in all of their celebrations of life's ongoing mysteries and rewards has given me an even deeper sense of what it will mean to sit down with my family and friends when my big day finally arrives later this year. And that is the happiest return I could ever imagine.

Acknowledgments

I am grateful to my parents, Jo Ann and Joseph Tutera, for their love and for teaching me the importance of family. They always celebrated our birthdays big . . . not with expensive parties or gifts, but with warm wishes and lots of laughter. To the rest of my family — Maria, Gregg, Amy, Rich, Mia, Richie, Vergie, and Scott — thank you for always being there to celebrate life with me.

To my loyal fans, thank you for your continued support and for encouraging me to do what I do best. I look forward to many more years of entertaining with you. I hope this book inspires you to celebrate your life in style!

To everyone who provided me with the materials to make this book as beautiful as I envisioned, from the creative cake designers to the companies that provided product, thank you for being part of this *Big Birthdays* party.

To Jennifer and Charles Maring, who capture my creations like no one else, thank you for your support, patience, and friendship.

To Eda Kalkay, my incredible publicist and equally incredibly friend, thank you for all you do for me. Your continued guidance, support, and sense of humor help me do my job to the fullest.

To my entire staff, thank you for all your hard work and dedication to this project. You all added your own special touches in making each birthday party come alive with excitement. Thank you, Allene Diana, Kate Gigler, Lucy Jolis, Lisa Munier, Sal Pontillo, David Razzano, and Steve Skopick.

A special thanks to Frederica Friedman, my amazing literary agent, for providing advice and guidance. To my editor, Kristen Schilo, thank you for always being a joy to work with and for adding laughter to the process. To Jill Cohen, my publisher, thank you for seeing my vision and what lies ahead. And to the entire Bulfinch team, thanks for making this project a reality.

To Ceridwen Morris, the most gifted writer, thank you for putting words to my creative vision. Your work and dedication mean so much to me. You are so much fun that you make the entire process feel like one big party!

And once again, to "my angel," Ryan Jurica, whose creativity is boundless and who touches my life in such a powerful way, thank you for your enduring support. Our bond makes sharing life feel like we are constantly celebrating life. It is our journey together that allows us to continue creating wonderful books like this one. I love you, Ryan!

Resources

Party Rental Ltd.
Locations in New York, New Jersey, Connecticut, Pennsylvania, Maryland, and Washington, D.C.
888-PR-HIPPO (888-774-4776)
www.partyrentalltd.com

1. CHLOE'S 1ST BIRTHDAY

"Pot Luck" Plates from Rosanna, Inc.
440 South Holgate Street
Seattle, WA 98134
206-264-7882 or 866-ROSANNA
www.rosannainc.com

Teddy Bears from Princess Soft Toys
7664 West 78th Street
Minneapolis, MN 55439
800-252-7638 or 952-829-5596
www.princesstoys.com

Sorbets from Ciao Bella Gelato
231 40th Street
Irvington, NJ 07111
973-373-1200 or 800-GELATO-3
www.ciaobellagelato.com

Cupcakes from Baked
359 Van Brunt Street
Brooklyn, NY 11231
718-222-0345
www.bakedshop.com
email: info@bakednyc.com

Invitations from Encore Studios
17 Industrial Street W.
Clifton, NJ 07012
800-526-0497x545
www.encorestudios.com

Cake Plates, Water Pitcher, and Glasses by L. E. Smith Glass for House Wear
266 7th Street
Hoboken, NJ 07030
201-659-6009
www.housewear.biz

Flatware from Horchow
877-944-9888
www.horchow.com

Baby Spoons from Villeroy and Boch
www.villeroy-boch.com

Bibs from VintageLily
9 Homer Street
Newport, RI 02840
401-207-3436 or 877-4BABYBIBS (877-422-2924)
www.vintagelily.com
email: info@vintagelily.com

High Chairs from IKEA
www.ikea.com

Monogrammed Sterling Baby Bracelets from Sticky Jewelry, Inc.
204 37th Avenue N., #127
St. Petersburg, FL 33704
727-823-9500; 866-204-3533 (fax)
www.stickyj.com
email: customerservice@stickyj.com

2. KEVIN'S 5TH BIRTHDAY

Wicker Stools from IKEA
www.ikea.com

Fishing Tackle, Lures, and Accessories
www.gofishin.com
www.chinalure.com

Carved Wooden Ducks, Shore Birds, and Decoys by Paul H. Umfleet for Wooden U Woodcarving
www.umfleet.net
email: mail@umfleet.net (orders)

Blue Flatware from Williams-Sonoma
877-812-6235
www.williams-sonoma.com
www.kitchenwareontheweb.com
www.replacements.com

"Acacia" Wood Chargers from Crate & Barrel
800-967-6696
www.crateandbarrel.com

Ceramic Fish Plates from Newport Nautical Decor, Inc.
P.O. Box 4122
Tulsa, OK 74159-0122
866-836-1046
www.newportnauticaldecor.com

Cake from Elegant Cheese Cakes
103–2 Harvard Avenue
Half Moon Bay, CA 94019
650-728-2248
www.elegantcheesecakes.com

3. LUCY'S 16TH BIRTHDAY

Location: Divine Studio
21 East 4th Street, Suite 605
New York, NY 10003
212-598-3060
www.divinestudio.com

Cake by Lisa Cornish for
Sweet Art Baking Company
556 Lacabana Beach Drive
Las Vegas, NV 89138
702-250-5444

"Napoleon" Flatware and "Haute
Shoes" Plates from Rosanna, Inc.
440 South Holgate Street
Seattle, WA 98134
206-264-7882 or 866-ROSANNA
www.rosannainc.com

Escort Cards by Esther Kartus for
Party Art LLC
5 Wildwood Drive
North Caldwell, NJ 07006
e-mail: partyart4you@aol.com

Invitations from Encore Studios
17 Industrial Street W.
Clifton, NJ 07012
800-526-0497x545
www.encorestudios.com

"Glam Girl Glasses" from
House Wear
266 7th Street
Hoboken, NJ 07030
201-659-6009
www.housewear.biz

Feather Boas from The
Feather Place
40 W. 38th Street, 3rd Floor
New York, NY 10018
212-921-4452
www.featherplace.com
email: websales@featherplace. com

4. DYLAN'S 25TH BIRTHDAY

Location: Crobar
530 West 28th Street
New York, NY 10001
212-629-9000
www.crobar.com

Ghost Candelabras by Jon
Russell for MoMa Store
11 West 53rd Street
New York, NY 10019
212-708-9700
The MoMa Mail Order Dept.
P.O. Box 2534
West Chester, PA 19380-0308
800-447-MoMA (800-447-6662)
www.momastore.org

Flutter Fetti from The Flutter
Fetti® Fun Factory
2925 Bienville Street
New Orleans, LA 70119
504-822-1336 or 877-321-1999
www.flutterfetti.com
email: info@flutterfetti.com

Purple, Orange, and Red "Amac"
Boxes from The Container Store
888-CONTAIN (888-266-8246)
www.containerstore.com

Glasses from Peàn Doubulyu
10 White Street
Pawtucket, RI 02860
401-726-4356
www.peandoubulyu.com

Cake by Cheryl Kleinman for
Cheryl Kleinman Cakes
448 Atlantic Avenue
Brooklyn, NY 11217
718-237-2271

Food by Chef Chris Daly for
Aroma
36 East 4th Street
New York, NY 10003
212-375-0100
www.aromanyc.com

Chair Rental from Arenson
Prop Center
396 10th Avenue at 33rd Street
New York, NY 10000
212-633-2400
www.aof.com

5. JOHN'S 30TH BIRTHDAY

Cake from Eleni's
75 9th Avenue (in the Chelsea
Market)
New York, NY 10011
212-255-7990
www.elenis.com

Crystals from Accent Decor Inc.
4000 Northfield Way, Unit 100
Roswell, GA 30076
800-385-5114 or 770-346-0707

Crystal Ropings and Beads from
Spectrum Home Furnishings
P.O. Box 922
Farmingdale, NJ 07727
800-668-3899
www.freedomcrystal.com
www.greatchandelier.com
email: spectrumhf@aol.com

"Sunburst" Chargers from Pier 1
Imports
800-245-4595 (customer service)
www.pier1.com

"Newgrange Platinum"
Dinnerware by Waterford Fine
China fromWaterford
Wedgwood USA
www.wwusa.com
www.wedgwood.com
www.waterford.com

"Ashmont" Sterling Flatware
from Reed & Barton
144 West Britannia Street
Taunton, MA 02780
800-343-1383 (customer service)
www.reedandbarton.com

Raspberry Chipotle Barbecue
Sauce by Tartare for Tartare
Catering, Butcher Shop, and
Prepared Foods
663 9th Avenue
New York, NY 10036
212-333-5300
www.tartare.com

6. ALLEYNE'S 40TH BIRTHDAY

Location: Highlands Country Club
955 Route 9D
Garrison, New York 10524
www.highlandscountryclub.net
845-424-3604

Food by Directing Chef Jeremy
Griffiths for the Highlands
Country Club
"Awnings Summer" Dinnerware
and "Summer" Glasses by Marc
Blackwell for Marc Blackwell New
York
157 West 26th Street
New York, New York 10001
212-696-2827; 866-755-6269 (customer service)
www.marcblackwell.com

Martini Glasses from Rosanna,
Inc.
440 South Holgate Street
Seattle, WA 98134
866-ROSANNA
www.rosannainc.com

Cake by Elissa Strauss for
Confetti Cakes
102 West 87th Street
New York, NY 10024
212-877-9580
www.confetticakes.com
email: cakedesigner@confetti-
cakes.com

Flatware from Ginkgo
International, Ltd.
8102 Lemont Road, Suite 1100
Woodridge, IL 60517
630-910-5244
www.ginkgoint.com
email: ginkgo@flash.net

Chocolates by Fauchon for
Fauchon Store and Café Fauchon
442 Park Avenue
New York, NY 10022
212-308-5919 or 866-784-7001 or
718-784-7001
www.fauchon.com

7. CYNTHIA'S 50TH BIRTHDAY

Cake by Buddy Valastro Jr. at
Carlo's Bakery
95 Washington Street
Hoboken, NJ 07030
201-659-3671
www.carlosbakery.com
e-mail: info@carlosbakery.com

Christmas Ornaments and Pearl
Strands
Hillcrest Garden
95 West Century Road
Paramus, NJ 07652-1428
800-437-7000 or 201-599-3030
www.hillcrestgarden.com
*(Wholesaler with Retail Referral
Available)*

Invitations from Encore Studios
800-526-0497x545
www.encorestudios.com

"Strata" Dinnerware and
Champagne Flute by Jasper
Conran for Jasper Conran at
Wedgwood
www.wedgwood.com
www.jasperconran.com

"Dane" Stainless Flatware from
Reed & Barton
144 West Britannia Street
Taunton, MA 02780
800-343-1383 (customer service)
www.reedandbarton.com

Alexandra Rosé Champagne
1990
from Laurent-Perrier
www.laurentperrierus.com

8. HOGAN'S 65TH BIRTHDAY

Cake from Mim J. Galligan
P.O. Box 104
Garrison, NY 10524
845-265-2328
www.mimgalligan.com

"Sumatra" Dinnerware and
"Espana" Glassware (Amber)
from ZGallerie
1855 West 139th Street
Gardena, CA 90249
800-358-8288 or 800-908-6748
www.ZGallerie.com (customer
service)

"Daniela" Flatware from Match, Inc.
201-792-9444
www.match1995.com

Invitations from Encore Studios
800-526-0497x545
www.encorestudios.com

"Tamarind" Chargers from Pier 1 Imports
800-245-4595
www.pier1.com

Candles and Votives from Zodax
14040 Arminta Street
Panorama City, CA 91402
818-785-5626 or 800-800-3443
www.zodax.com
email: info@zodax.com

9. GLORIA'S 75TH BIRTHDAY

"Eric's Time" Dinner Plates by Marc Blackwell for Marc Blackwell New York
157 West 26th Street
New York, NY 10001
212-696-2827; 866-755-6269 (customer service)
www.marcblackwell.com

Crystal Glasses from Saint-Louis (Collection: Grand Lieu, Cosmos, and Bubbles)
800-238-5522 (customer service)

"Solid Teak Lutyers Benches" and "Solid Teak Round Back Side Chairs" from Wood Classics
47 Steve's Lane
Gardiner, NY 12525
800-385-0030
www.woodclassics.com

Cake by Florian Bellanger for Fauchon Store and Café Fauchon
442 Park Avenue
New York, NY 10022
212-308-5919 or 866-784-7001
www.fauchon.com

Mini Apple Pies from the Little Pie Company
407 West 14th Street
New York, NY 10014
212-414-2324
www.littlepiecompany.com

Invitations from Encore Studios
800-526-0497x545
www.encorestudios.com

"Chantilly" Gold Sterling Flatware from Gorham
800-4GORHAM (800-446-7426)
www.gorham1831.com

French Antique Iron Chandeliers from ABC Carpet & Home
888 Broadway
New York, NY 10003
212-473-3000
www.abchome.com

Food by Chef Jeremy Griffiths (New York, NY)

10. JO ANN & JOE'S 100TH BIRTHDAY

Dinnerware, Flatware, Glasses, and Canister from Match, Inc.
201-792-9444
www.match1995.com

Antique Chairs from ABC Carpet & Home
888 Broadway
New York, NY 10003
212-473-3000
www.abchome.com

Cake by Charmaine Jones for Cakediva
720 Monroe Street
Hoboken, NJ 07030
212-722-0678 or 201-216-0123
www.cakediva.com
e-mail: cakediva@aol.com

Food by Chef Martin Czelder for Tartare Catering, Butcher Shop, and Prepared Foods
653 9th Avenue
New York, NY 10036
212-333-5300
www.tartare.com

Menu Cards and Place Cards designed by Chrissy Carter
201-240-9634

Invitations from Encore Studios
800-526-0497x545
www.encorestudios.com

Yellow, Green, and Orange M&M's in Match Glass Canister
www.mms.com

Index